gather together

"*Gather Together* warmly celebrates the reality that nurturing our souls in community is as necessary as nourishing our bodies at mealtime. The menus of good food and thoughtful reflections Catherine Fowler Sample has crafted are a much-needed invitation to reenter into the intimacy we humans crave. Her recipes are written as a warm, approachable invitation to make good use of the gifts we've been given, and her stories draw us into a modern take on an age-old truth: to gather as a community is essential; to be together in the Lord is to thrive. The book is intentional, purposeful, and fruitful in more ways than one."

Lindsay Schlegel
Author of *Don't Forget to Say Thank You*

"As someone who has only recently fallen in love with time in the kitchen, *Gather Together* has been the perfect book to inspire cooking adventures and to make time and room for people to join us for dinner parties. I love this book because it's filled with wonderful stories, easy and delicious recipes, and the perfect template for how to build friendships and community around a good meal. Grab your apron, fire up the oven, and get to cooking: people are coming over and *Gather Together* will help you prepare!

Katie Prejean McGrady
International Catholic speaker, author, and host of the *Ave Explores* podcast

"Catherine Fowler Sample serves up story after story highlighting the blessed necessity of gathering around the table and removes virtually every obstacle to it by providing twelve full-blown menus with easy-to-follow recipes. Each chapter offers you bite-sized spiritual morsels that will whet your appetite for more of God and for more connection with those you love around the table."

Jeff Young
Founder and producer of *The Catholic Foodie* blog and podcast

"*Gather Together* encourages me as a priest and chef. It shows that more people are understanding the power of food and how it can heal, strengthen, and nourish what is most important about the food—namely, the people we serve. It's my hope that this book becomes another recipe book, not just for a meal but a recipe to follow on Christ's commandment to love one another."

Rev. Leo E. Patalinghug
International speaker, author, and creator of the Food and Faith Movement

gather together

RECIPES AND REFLECTIONS TO INSPIRE FAITH AND FRIENDSHIP AROUND THE TABLE

CATHERINE FOWLER SAMPLE

AVE MARIA PRESS AVE Notre Dame, Indiana

Founded in 1865, Ave Maria Press is a ministry of the United States Province of Holy Cross.

www.avemariapress.com

Paperback: ISBN-13 978-1-59471-971-4

E-book: ISBN-13 978-1-59471-972-1

Cover image © Brad and Jen Butcher/Stocksy.

Interior illustrations © 2016–2019 Maryna Mykhalska.

Cover and text design by Brianna Dombo.

Printed and bound in the United States of America.

Library of Congress Cataloging-in-Publication Data
Names: Sample, Catherine Fowler, author.
Title: Gather together : recipes and reflections to inspire faith and friendship around the table / Catherine Fowler Sample.
Description: Notre Dame, Indiana : Ave Maria Press, 2020. | Includes bibliographical references. | Summary: "In Gather Together, Catherine Fowler Sample offers meditations on faith, friendship, and community and more than forty recipes, all for Catholics who crave authentic connection, fun gatherings, and good food"-- Provided by publisher.
Identifiers: LCCN 2020023860 (print) | LCCN 2020023861 (ebook) | ISBN 9781594719714 (paperback) | ISBN 9781594719721 (ebook)
Subjects: LCSH: Dinners and dining--Religious aspects--Catholic Church. | Cookbooks. | Christian life--Catholic authors.
Classification: LCC BR115.N87 S26 2020 (print) | LCC BR115.N87 (ebook) | DDC 248.4/6--dc23
LC record available at https://lccn.loc.gov/2020023860
LC ebook record available at https://lccn.loc.gov/2020023861

to my dad and mom,
for a lifetime of
gathering memories.

to my husband,
for the new ones we're
making together.

Wherever the Catholic sun doth shine,
there's always laughter and good red wine.
At least I've always found it so.
Benedicamus Domino!

—Hilaire Belloc

Contents

Introduction

Julia Child wisely said, "Cooking is one failure after another, and that's how you finally learn." I can attest to this truth! And upon reflection, I've realized it applies brilliantly to the spiritual life as well. Food—and therefore cooking—has a deeply spiritual component, especially for Catholics because we believe that Christ offers himself to us as our daily bread.

To make food is to care for the body at the most basic level because we all need to eat. But it can also tend to a higher emotional need—if we take the next step and share the food we've made, giving someone undivided attention at the same table. The preparation, offering, and sharing of food is elevated to a spiritual practice and an act of love.

This book celebrates food, faith, and fellowship. Many times we desire to deepen our connection with God and one another, but struggle to find the time due to hectic day-to-day busyness. This book is an invitation to slow down and make time to gather: Read a reflection. Make a meal. Share it with those you love. Cultivate intentional environments to grow with others in your Catholic faith.

Some of the sweetest moments of my life have involved gatherings centered on meals: family dinners during childhood, date nights with my husband, holiday reunions, gathering with friends, or lunching with sisters. Yet when I think back on all these treasured times, the food itself cannot hold a candle to the bonds of communion that were built. So much of feeding the body is, in fact, feeding the soul. This is why I love the concept of combining the two genres of cookbook and spiritual reflections.

On a spiritual level, the reflections in this book are intended to support faith and fellowship among Catholic young people, encouraging connections with family, friends, or fellow parishioners. There are twelve chapters, one for each month of the year. Each month has a suggested theme for a gathering, along with a prayer and conversation prompts to help gatherings get off to a great start. Of course, the reflections can serve as individual enrichment, but the power of gathering is unique. Christ himself said, "For where two or three are gathered together in my name, there am I in the midst of them" (Mt 18:20). I have seen how good a simple faith-based gathering can be. It can be the first time a newcomer feels at home in a community, it can provide a launching pad for new friendships, it can open a door for career opportunities, and at the very least, it can be a fun time.

I learned to cook from my mother. She can make flaming Christmas puddings, fried chicken that rivals the best in the South (and we're not even from the South), and brownies that are the most delicious of any I've ever tried. Her number-one lesson in the kitchen is empowering: anyone can cook. Now, this comes with three caveats: never substitute ingredients (allergies aside), always season food, and read the recipe at least twice before you start. Through the years, I have followed her advice, and I have had my own successes in the kitchen, curating a set of tried-and-true recipes that deliver time and again. This book features some of these recipes, providing twelve sets of meals for eight guests, but each can easily be cut in half for a smaller group. Utilize the recipes to supplement some of your own favorites, or allow them to take the guesswork out of menu planning when you want to serve others.

While it's true that cooking can be fun, let's be real—it's work. I wish I could say I am a person who loves cooking to decompress, but I often have to motivate myself to make dinner after working a long day. One night in particular, I was feeling pretty tired and was waffling back and forth about asking my husband to pick something up on his way home from the office. In the end, I decided to go ahead and make dinner because I had all the ingredients for Sonora chicken pasta. After we had finished dinner, we were sitting at the table when my husband said, "Wow, this was so nice to come home to. Thank you." It was so special to hear those words, and it really put making a meal into perspective: it was work, and it was worth it. The same goes for gathering. It takes effort and energy to host a special get-together, but the results build relationships and beautiful memories.

I wrote this book before the coronavirus upended daily life for most of us in the United States, and it has quickly become clear that gathering together is a privilege we may never take for granted again. If there comes a time when group gatherings aren't possible for you, I'd encourage you to use this book as a springboard for creatively connecting with your household, roommates, or far-away family and friends. You could make the recipes with loved ones over video chat, or plan an evening of reflection by phone based on the questions and prayer prompts. While distance makes forming community more challenging, the consistency of intentional connection can be a unique balm during uncertain times.

I pray this book serves as a conduit for God's love, comfort, and nourishment—and that you will take it and be a conduit for the same graces to your circle of influence. May you experience the richness of preparing food for the ones you love, grow deeper in devotion to God, and make time to gather together.

Shine on,
Catherine
Feast of the Annunciation, 2020

CHAPTER 1

Walk On Securely

For we walk by faith, not by sight.

—2 Corinthians 5:7

I moved to Southern California when I was a fresh-faced twenty-year-old. I was transferring to a new college, but it may as well have been a transfer to another planet. The West Coast was radically different from my landlocked hometown in the Heartland, and I barely knew a soul there aside from Great-Aunt Patsy. This early January in SoCal was unlike any other I had experienced: The sun was warm. The sky was blue. Jacaranda trees were filled with amethyst blooms. Although it was winter, it smelled of spring, and the world was full of possibility—a mingling of trepidation and hope.

In a new environment, I couldn't help but take in the world with fresh eyes and live differently. When I was outside, I slowed down and stopped to smell the roses (quite literally!). For school, I signed up for classes that I actually wanted to take instead of stressing about requirements. For my body, I walked everywhere. For my heart, I took more time to pray. I had long-term goals before me, and yet I was tranquil.

A decade later, I experienced a January that was the polar opposite. I had moved with my husband to the East Coast, where the weather was cold and dreary, and we were undergoing a rocky transition to parenthood. We were blessed with a beautiful baby girl, but she was suffering from terrible colic. It made us so sad that we couldn't make her feel better when she cried. My husband was a rock of strength and patience through it all, but I felt as if I were on an emotional roller coaster. As I reflected on this changing season in our life, I read from the writings of St. Clare of Assisi, and I was struck by her mantra of *vade secura,* which means "walk on securely," or trusting in God's providence.

Dwelling on this phrase helped me understand why my first SoCal January was so wonderful. It wasn't the beautiful surroundings; it was the spirit in which I lived—I was walking securely in God's providence. I needed to reconnect with that spirit and bring it into my new-mom East Coast life.

And yet, I realized that to walk on securely in God's providence doesn't mean that we are disconnected from our humanity. It's not acting as if everything is great when you are going through a tough time, but it's walking in his grace despite difficulties. In this regard, I found a model in St. Clare as well, particularly in how she reacted to the death of St. Francis of Assisi. She was very heartbroken when he died because not only was she one of his first followers—and the founder of the sister order to the Franciscans, the Poor Clares—but she became one of his dearest friends.

This is the reflection a friend shared with me:

> [Clare] cried and kept little remembrances, but she went on. She had the full human response enlarged into the divine response. She didn't say, "I can't go on without him," or "What shall become of us?" She said that, after God, he was their only pillar and support, but now the pillar and support is taken away; we have God alone. And she went on. . . . It seems to me that if we are not capable of the valid human response, we cannot arrive at the divine response. She did not step over this. She knew how to cry, she knew how to laugh, and she knew which response was appropriate. Then it was enlarged into the divine response.[1]

This idea of having an appropriate human response transformed into a divine response warmed my heart. I found it so honest and real. It bolstered my courage to push on—to walk on securely. I was able to better acknowledge my current feelings and view them through the lens of God's providence.

Thinking in terms of transforming a human response into a divine response offered a different perspective as my husband and I went through the time of trial with our baby daughter because it challenged me to trust in God's providence despite not being able to see the end results. I saw the beauty of waiting on God to bring good out of difficulty, which he inevitably does, even if it is not in the way we would imagine or in our time frame. I saw it as an opportunity to grow closer to him. In the midst of my daughter's crying, I too cried out to him. I told him my feelings and fears. I made time to pray the Rosary, which is a beautiful and grounding form of meditation. I found that after I prayed the Rosary things were better. It was as if I was seeing the world through Ros*ary*-colored glasses. Meditating on the life of Christ and the model of faith we have in the Blessed Virgin took me out of myself. Sometimes I would pray for a specific person on each bead, which reminded me that so many people have gone through difficulties, and so many people need prayers—not just me! This way of praying helped me transform my response into a divine response, and it helped me and my husband to put our walking shoes on and embrace the cross that we were being asked to carry.

Now, more than two years later, the colic days are in the rearview mirror, and we are reveling in the joys of parenthood as we watch our little girl grow by the day. I credit getting through that rough patch to my husband's goodwill, visits from my mom and sisters, and St. Clare. Walking on securely offered a perspective that was eluding me. We live in an age where we are encouraged to eliminate problems instead of working through them. Our fast-paced world doesn't make walking seem glamorous. Our lives are fueled by rushing to the next thing: whether it's the hurry of retail stores setting up for Christmas in August, the push to overschedule our lives, the pressure to post something that will get more likes than last time, or the need to respond to every notification from our phone. The list runs on—and runs us ragged.

The practice of walking on securely (albeit imperfectly) has made me recognize my exhaustion and the futility of sprinting from one thing to the next. When I find myself tempted to fly toward what is ahead, the call to *vade secura* brings me back down to earth, and I find myself happier, more secure, and able to treasure the present and precious moments.

Prayer for Gathering

A blessing from St. Clare's second letter to Blessed Agnes of Prague

What you hold may you always hold.
What you do, may you always do and never abandon.
But with swift pace, light step, and unswerving feet,
so that even your steps stir up no dust,
go forward; the spirit of our God has called you. Amen.

Conclude by saying the Our Father.

Prompts for Conversation

- Was there a significant time in your life when you "walked on securely" in God's providence?
- How have the times when you have "walked on securely" made you feel compared to times when you have not?
- Is there a part of your life that needs to slow to a walk? What would that look like? How can you do it?

Menu: Soup for a Group

Hosting a January Soup Group fits perfectly into the spirit of slowing to a steady and secure walk—with God and with one another. Making time for quality time is no small feat. It requires us to be secure in God's providence and to set aside whatever seemingly important tasks we have, in order to focus on creating a meal for loved ones to gather around and be present to one another. Such an occasion allows us to share our human responses to what life is throwing at us, and then glean wisdom from others as to how our situations fit into the larger divine response. What better way to connect in this way than over a warm cup of soup?

Starter: Sweet Pea Pesto Dip
Main: Italian Soup
Side: Garlic Bread
Dessert: Cannoli Bites

STARTER: SWEET PEA PESTO DIP

Serves 8

I love this dip because it can be made in advance. Serve with tasty crackers or veggies of your choice—carrot sticks or cherry tomatoes speared with long toothpicks make for easy dipping!

Ingredients You'll Need

1 bag frozen sweet peas (10 ounces), thawed
1 garlic clove, minced or pressed
2 tablespoons lemon juice (1 lemon)
1 cup fresh basil, lightly packed
1/2 cup toasted pine nuts
1 teaspoon sea salt

1/4 teaspoon black pepper, freshly ground
2 tablespoons extra virgin olive oil
Crackers or veggies of choice for dipping

Tools You'll Need

Colander or a large mixing bowl and resealable plastic bag
Food processor or blender
Knife
Cutting board
Garlic press (optional)

How to Make It

1. Begin thawing the frozen peas. To do this, empty frozen peas into a strainer or colander and run cool water over them until thawed. This should take around 10 minutes. You will know they are thawed when you can take a pea and squish it easily. Another option is to place the peas in a resealable bag and submerge them in a large bowl of cold water until thawed, which will take around 30 minutes.

2. Take a garlic clove and remove the sheath (the papery skin a piece of garlic is wrapped in). You can approach the garlic in a few ways. You could use a garlic press, or you could finely chop it with a knife on a cutting board. If you plan to use a food processor for this recipe, you could place the garlic clove in the food processor and set it to chop until the garlic clove is pulverized into small bits. This should take around 30 seconds.

3. Use the knife and cutting board to cut the lemon in half. Squeeze the lemon halves to get 2 tablespoons of juice. Then add the juice, thawed peas, basil, pine nuts, salt, and pepper into the food processor or blender. Process for around 30–60 seconds.

4. When the ingredients are blended to a smooth consistency, and processor or blender is off, scrape the sides. Start processing again, adding the olive oil in small increments. Most of the time, a food processor or blender will have little holes in the top so you can add the olive oil in a thin stream while running the processor. Blend until the olive oil is fully incorporated and the mixture looks smooth.

5. Taste for seasoning, and if need be, add more salt, pepper, and lemon juice.

Recipe Notes

- Make ahead: This sweet pea pesto can be made in advance and refrigerated for up to 3 days. Take out 20 minutes prior to serving in order to reach room temperature for best taste.
- There's no need to buy a fancy food processor—although if you have one, that is great! I am still using an old, two-chop-setting food processor that I have had for about a decade, and it always gets the job done.
- When you buy basil, do not refrigerate it, because that makes it wilt.

 # MAIN: ITALIAN SOUP

Serves 8

This soup is outta-this-world good. It's great for feeding a crowd for a soup group (which I've done once or twice!). It is also perfect to make on a Sunday night in advance for Monday dinner, and then have it for lunch during the rest of the week. (I had this down to a science when I was single.) This soup is also extra special to me because it was the first meal I ever made my husband when we were dating. Maybe a way to a man's heart is through a good soup!

Ingredients You'll Need

1 pound spicy Italian sausage, uncooked
1 onion, chopped
2 cloves garlic, minced or pressed
1 (32-ounce) box beef broth
1 (15-ounce) can crushed tomatoes, such as Dei Fratelli
1 (15-ounce) can diced tomatoes, fire roasted
1 (15-ounce) can tomato sauce
1 cup dry red wine, such as Cabernet Sauvignon
3 carrots, chopped
1 tablespoon granulated sugar
2 teaspoons Italian seasoning
1 (10-ounce) package cheese tortellini (found in the refrigerated section at store)

3 small zucchini, chopped
1 cup Parmesan cheese, grated or shaved

Tools You'll Need

Dutch oven or soup pot that will hold at least 5 1/2 quarts
Heatproof spoon or meat turner
Plate
Heat-safe container for grease
Knife
Cutting board
Garlic press (optional)
Wine corkscrew
Can opener

How to Make It

1. Turn your stove top on to medium-high. Remove sausage from casing and place into the Dutch oven or the soup pot you plan to use to cook the soup. Break apart the sausage links with a heatproof spoon or meat turner. Add the chopped onion and garlic. Brown the sausage until no pink remains, which will take 8–10 minutes. When finished browning, remove the sausage-onion-garlic mixture to a plate, and drain grease into a heat-safe container to discard later. Always be very careful when doing this, and never pour grease down your sink drain—it will cool, harden, and clog your drain.

2. Once the grease has been drained, toss the sausage mixture back into the Dutch oven or soup pot you were previously using and add the beef broth, crushed tomatoes, fire-roasted diced tomatoes, tomato sauce, wine, carrots, sugar, and Italian seasoning. Bring to a boil, and then turn down to simmer for 30 minutes.

3. At the 30-minute mark, add tortellini and chopped zucchini, and let simmer for another 30 minutes. Ideally you'll add these ingredients 40 minutes before you're ready to serve.

4. When finished, allow the soup to cool for 10 minutes. If you don't want to wait (like me!), you can add 1 to 2 ice cubes to individual serving bowls; otherwise, the soup will be too hot to eat right away!

5. Serve with grated or shaved Parmesan for garnish and garlic bread as the side.

Recipe Notes

- Make ahead: The soup can be made the night before. Once soup has been removed from the hot stove top and cooled a bit (around 20 minutes), you can transfer it to a container to store in the fridge. I usually refrigerate it in the Dutch oven I used to make the soup, which cuts down on dishes and also makes for easy reheating. Prior to the meal, place soup on stove top and set to medium heat for 15–20 minutes, stirring occasionally until heated through.
- Dietary considerations: To modify for gluten-free guests, try DePuma's tortellini or Udi's Gluten Free Pesto Tortellini. To modify for dairy-free guests, do not serve with tortellini (cheese-free tortellini is next to impossible to find). Serving without tortellini does not change how good this soup is! For the Parmesan, offer a dairy-free Parmesan-style cheese alternative.
- Buying uncooked sausage is key to the flavor of this soup. Precooked sausage will not create the same flavor effect.
- Use grated or shaved Parmesan depending on what you prefer. Shaved will produce stringy cheese in the hot soup, and grated will melt in.

SIDE: GARLIC BREAD

Serves 8

This garlic bread is a snap to make and rivals that of a restaurant. Brace for compliments.

Ingredients You'll Need

    1 loaf of French bread
    1/2 cup salted butter, softened
    3 garlic cloves, minced or pressed
    1 teaspoon Italian seasoning
    1/2 cup Parmesan cheese, grated

Tools You'll Need

Aluminum foil
Baking sheet
Knife
Cutting board
Garlic press (optional)
Small mixing bowl
Silicone spatula

How to Make It

1. Preheat oven to 400 degrees Fahrenheit.
2. Place a sheet of aluminum foil on a baking sheet. Set aside.
3. Using a knife and cutting board, slice the French bread loaf in half lengthwise.
4. To make the garlic spread, take a small bowl and combine the butter, garlic, Italian seasoning, and grated Parmesan using a spatula. Stir together vigorously until incorporated and smooth.
5. Spread the mixture onto the sliced loaf of bread.
6. Place bread on the prepared baking sheet and bake for 12 minutes, or until golden. For additional crisp, set oven to broil for 30 seconds at the very end, but watch carefully so as not to burn, because it can happen fast!
7. Remove garlic bread from oven and cut each length of bread into fourths to yield more generous slices (and one should always be generous with garlic bread!).

Recipe Notes

- Make ahead: The garlic spread can be made a day ahead and stored covered at room temperature until you are ready to make the garlic bread.

DESSERT:
CANNOLI BITES

Serves 8 (Recipe makes enough for everyone to have 4–6 as they are small.)
A fun, bite-sized twist on the traditional cannoli, these are perfect to round out this menu's Italian theme. These treats need to be prepared ahead of a gathering, but it's best to assemble no further in advance than the morning of the event. These little bites are always a big hit!

Ingredients You'll Need

For Cannoli Cups
> 2 premade pie crusts, thawed (These are found in the freezer section and come in packs of two.)
> 2 tablespoons all-purpose flour
> 1/4 cup granulated sugar
> 2 teaspoons ground cinnamon
> 1/8 teaspoon ground nutmeg

For Cannoli Filling
> 12 ounces whole-milk ricotta cheese
> 8 ounces mascarpone cheese
> 1/2 cup powdered sugar (This is not "regular" granulated sugar.)

For Toppings
> 1/2 cup semi-sweet chocolate chips, for melting
> Oil (When melting chocolate chips, if you add a dash of cooking oil like coconut, sunflower, or extra light olive oil, it will keep sauce from burning or drying out.)
> 1/3 cup mini semi-sweet chocolate chips
> Pistachios, finely chopped
> Flaked coconut, sweetened
> Sprinkles
> Powdered sugar for dusting

Tools You'll Need

> Medium mixing bowl
> Spoon or silicone spatula
> Measuring cups

Measuring spoons
Sifter (optional)
Plastic wrap
Large cutting board or parchment paper
Rolling pin (optional)
2 1/2-inch round biscuit cutter, or a similar-sized cookie cutter, or a
    juice glass and knife
Mini muffin tin
Knife (optional)
Cutting board (optional)
Small saucepan or microwave-safe dish
Heatproof spoon
Wire cooling rack
Large resealable plastic bag

How to Make It

1. Preheat your oven to 425 degrees Fahrenheit.
2. Start with the filling because it needs to chill for 30 minutes. Add the
    ricotta and mascarpone cheese to a mixing bowl and combine by hand
    with a spoon or spatula until smooth. Sift in the 1/2 cup of powdered
    sugar and mix; if you don't have a sifter, stir a little longer until there
    are no lumps. Cover the filling and chill at least 30 minutes.
3. Take out your thawed pie crusts and spread them out on a lightly
    floured surface such as a large cutting board or even a large piece of
    parchment paper, which is what I often use.
4. Mix together the sugar, cinnamon, and nutmeg. Sprinkle this mixture
    across the top of the pie crusts, and gently press in with a rolling pin
    or your hands.
5. Take your biscuit cutter, or if you don't have one, use the top of a juice
    glass or a glass that is about 2 1/2 inches around. If all else fails, cut by
    hand with a sharp knife. The circles don't need to be perfect, but need
    to be big enough to go all the way up the sides of the muffin tin. You
    should get at least 48 circles total from the 2 pie crusts.
6. Take your mini muffin tin (do not grease with butter or spray with
    cooking spray), and lightly press each round into the muffin well, mak-
    ing sure the dough goes all the way up the sides.

7. Bake the cups in a 425-degree oven for 10 minutes or until the top edges of the cups are golden. Set on a cooling rack to cool completely, about 15 minutes.

8. To make a total of 48 cannoli cups, repeat the process with the remaining dough and bake a second batch. This will provide up to 6 cups per guest (and likely extras for people to take home!).

9. When the cups are cooling, take out your toppings. If using pistachios, finely chop them (they do not have to be super fine, but should be in crumbles).

10. Now, in a small saucepan over the stove top or in microwave-safe dish in the microwave, melt some chocolate chips with a dollop of coconut oil (or oil of your choice) for around 30 seconds. Stir with a heatproof spoon.

11. Then dip the top edge of each cup into the chocolate and whatever topping you choose of the pistachios, coconut flakes, or sprinkles. Allow the chocolate toppings to set at least 30 minutes at room temperature, or you can stick them in the freezer to harden for 5 minutes.

12. Once it is set, take the filling and spoon it into a large resealable bag. Cut the tip off one of the corners. This will be your piping bag. Pipe the cannoli filling into the cups a generous 3/4 of the way to the top and sprinkle with the mini chocolate chips, finishing off with a dusting of powdered sugar. Store in fridge until ready to serve.

CHAPTER 2

The Heart of Dating

My vocation is love.

—St. Thérèse of Lisieux

Do you want to go on a . . . date?

Despite the ever-increasing ways people are connecting these days, the good old-fashioned date seems to find itself at the bottom of the pile. As a woman who spent the "defining decade" of her twenties working in the film industry of Los Angeles (aptly dubbed the worst city to be single), I have firsthand knowledge regarding the matter! I found that amid the trends of texting, social media, hanging out, and hooking up, it wasn't a snap to find that quality relationship—you know, the kind of guy that's bring-home-for-Thanksgiving worthy.

This collapse of courtship culture fully dawned on me when I was at a friend's birthday party made up of more than a dozen women in their twenties and thirties. I looked around and realized every girl was single. There's not anything wrong with being single, but I knew for a fact that a majority of these ladies were interested in a relationship. This was my tipping point. I was determined to do something about dating culture and not just engage in the zillionth chat about what was wrong with it. I wanted to get to the heart of what was going on in the world of love and relationships. And so the idea for a documentary was born: *The Dating Project*.

It was a fascinating journey to write and produce a movie that was all about dating, and although I had preconceived notions about what had gone awry in the dating game, I wanted to set those aside as much as possible to learn from others—and did I ever. We filmed all over the United

15

States and heard stories from people in big cities and small towns, but no matter where we went, *everyone* was willing to discuss dating—in depth and on camera. Interview after interview confirmed that people wanted to bring back the date. People wished to experience more dates; people found it unfortunate that dating is considered old-fashioned; people were over "Netflix and chill"; people craved real conversations; people were sick of being swiped through like they didn't matter; people were exhausted by the social-media mind games.

After listening to so many individuals' stories on dating, it became clear to me that wanting to go on a date was just the tip of the emotional iceberg. Under the surface desire for a good date was a deeper desire to experience a real connection. My theory was proven true throughout the filming process and was well-illustrated when one of the single people filmed for the movie, Chris, a man in his forties, told the following story:

> Do I ever regret not being married? Well, I don't know what I don't know. I regret being an idiot and being a coward and not being true to myself. That's what I regret. You know. It's taken a little while to grow up. The "grass is greener" syndrome is a big one. And it's like if I look in the mirror, I'm thinking, *I'm putting things on people that I could never; I'm expecting that of somebody else that I could never do.* It's like, well, if I am looking at the menu all the time, it's just—how can I be in a relationship? . . . I was in New York about a year ago. I was on a commuter ferry and my phone died. I had been posting really funny things on Facebook and all these really cool sights, and when my phone died this tremendous sense of loneliness came over me. It really hit me like a deep loneliness. And then I realized that I wanna have a friend with me. I wanna be with someone. I wanna have a real connection.[1]

Yes, this was the big discovery: the yearning for a real connection goes far beyond romance and demands the courage to step outside the prevailing social script of disconnection.

This disconnection is embodied in the dating world by hookup culture. Now, at first I thought of hookup culture as limited to college-party material, but I have come to define hookup culture as a much broader spectrum of actions related to objectifying others and treating them as disposable. It can mean anything from treating sex as if it's not meant to take place within a sacrament, to ghosting someone you've been texting, to ignoring the person who is talking to you by being on your phone. It fosters a culture of disconnection that is devastating.

So much of relationship building involves nonsexual intimacy. True intimacy is being able to form and maintain a lasting connection with someone, built on mutual respect, trust, and support. This can be practiced through something as simple as eating together as a family, or asking someone out. Put your phone down. Have a conversation. Tune into the other person. Believe you are worth someone's time. Treat that person as you would hope someone would treat your sister or brother.

Another moment that really struck me while creating *The Dating Project* was when the young man in college was on cloud nine after his first date. The experience was clearly novel, even though it simply entailed going out for a burger with someone for about an hour. He said he wouldn't have spent the hour any other way, and for me this was proof positive that dating is more than "just dating." It's a validation of people's dignity, a chance to hold up a mirror to another person and allow their self-worth to shine through. What's truly beautiful is that this can happen over coffee!

In a happy turn of events I ended up getting to know an amazing man over coffee—whom I did bring to my family's Thanksgiving, and it was then that he asked my dad for permission to marry me. We experienced the power of real connection when we dated, and I can say that as we celebrate four years of marriage, real connection is what a relationship is all about. This real connection is the heart of dating. It comes in phases and builds over time, and it can be scary because eventually it does require all of you. In a world that prizes radical independence, it can feel intimidating to rely on someone else, to lean in on them, to be real with them, and to have them do the same with you. It requires something of you, but the return on investment is rich—the return on investment is real love.

Prayer for Gathering

From The Miraculous Invocation to St. Thérèse the Little Flower[2]

Give me childlike faith, to see the Face of God in the people and experiences of my life, and to love God with full confidence. Amen.

Conclude by saying the Our Father.

Prompts for Conversation

- What are your thoughts on this quote from the musical *Les Miserables*: "To love another person is to see the face of God."
- In what ways do you find it easy to form a real connection with those you meet?
- What are your roadblocks to experiencing real connection?

Menu: Sit-Down Dinner for Eight

The following menu includes short ribs, which I consider the perfect "fancy" dinner main, paired with pappardelle, a balsamic salad, and New Orleans Strawberries for dessert. Fair warning: the dish does take time to make, but there's a big payoff, and most of the work is done in the oven! You won't be slaving over the stove when people come over, because the short ribs are prepared the night before, rest in the refrigerator overnight so the flavors can meld and marry, and are reheated the next day before guests arrive. This is the ideal menu for a gathering where the food will be individually plated and you want a little wow-factor. Of course, it's romantic to have a dinner for two, but a sit-down gathering for eight has its beauty too!

Starter: Balsamic-Pepper Salad
Main and Side: Short Ribs in Tomato Sauce
with Pappardelle Pasta
Dessert: New Orleans Strawberries

STARTER:
BALSAMIC-PEPPER SALAD

Serves 8

I love homemade salad dressings for a few reasons: they are a breeze to whisk together, you can tailor exactly to taste, and you avoid all of the preservatives that come with so many store-bought options. After years of tinkering with different dressing ratios of vinegar, sugar, salt, and pepper, I landed on this winning combination. The flavor base is unique due to having more pepper than salt, which gives it an ever-so-slightly spicy flavor, but that is kept in check by the mildness of the Parmesan and the sweetness of the sugar. It pairs well with so many dishes and offers an especially nice contrast to the richness of the short ribs.

Ingredients You'll Need

   2 (9-ounce) bags salad, such as romaine or mixed greens

For Dressing

   2/3 cup extra virgin olive oil

   6 tablespoons balsamic vinegar (red wine vinegar or rice vinegar will
      work too)

   4 tablespoons Parmesan cheese, grated

   2 teaspoons granulated sugar

   2 teaspoons black pepper, freshly ground

   1 1/2 teaspoons sea salt

   1/2 teaspoon garlic powder

Tools You'll Need

   Serving bowl
   Whisk

How to Make It

1. Add all of the ingredients for the salad dressing to the serving bowl you
    plan to use for the salad (this saves on dishes later!), and whisk together
    thoroughly.
2. Immediately before serving add salad and toss.

Recipe Notes

• Make ahead: You can make this dressing in advance and store in the
   refrigerator for up to two weeks.
• Cut this recipe in half when serving only four people, or you can save
   the extra dressing in the fridge.

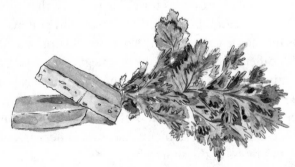

MAIN AND SIDE: SHORT RIBS IN TOMATO SAUCE WITH PAPPARDELLE PASTA

Adapted from Ree Drummond: "Braised Short Ribs"[3]
Serves 8
Time Note: 4 1/2 hours, plus time to sit in fridge overnight

Ingredients You'll Need

1 onion, diced
4 cloves garlic, minced or pressed
8 whole bone-in beef short ribs
4 whole boneless beef short ribs (See recipe notes.)
2 tablespoons olive oil
Sea salt and freshly ground black pepper, for seasoning
1 tablespoon brown sugar
1 (28-ounce) can crushed tomatoes, fire-roasted, such as Dei Fratelli
1 (15.5-ounce) can tomato sauce
1 cup red wine, preferably a dry red like Cabernet Sauvignon
1 teaspoon sea salt
1/2 teaspoon Italian seasoning
1/4 teaspoon red pepper flakes
1 pound pappardelle pasta
Parmesan cheese, shaved (for garnish)
Fresh parsley, chopped (for garnish)

Tools You'll Need

5 1/2 quart Dutch oven
Tongs
Heat-safe container for grease
Large pot or pan for cooking the pasta
Knife
Cutting board
Garlic press (optional)
Can opener
Measuring spoons
Wine corkscrew

How to Make It

1. Preheat oven to 275 degrees Fahrenheit.
2. Chop the onion and prep the garlic. Set aside.
3. Place the short ribs on a large plate or cutting board and season generously on both sides with salt and pepper. If you want to avoid dirtying dishes or dealing with a cutting board with raw meat, you can season them while they are still in the package.
4. In the Dutch oven, heat olive oil over medium-high heat until it starts to shimmer.
5. Sear the short ribs in the heated oil for 2 minutes on each side until they are slightly browned. You may need to do this in batches so as not to overcrowd the ribs. Set the browned ribs aside on a plate.
6. Before you discard the oil into a heat-safe dish, save a small portion (enough to lightly coat the bottom of the pan in order to cook the onions and garlic). When discarding the excess hot oil, always use extreme caution! Also, a friendly reminder to never pour grease down your sink drain as it will harden and clog the drain.
7. When excess oil has been removed from the Dutch oven, return to medium-high heat. Add garlic and onions, stirring for 2 minutes. Then add crushed tomatoes, tomato sauce, wine, salt, Italian seasoning, and red pepper flakes. Stir to combine.
8. Using tongs, add short ribs into the sauce until they are covered. Place lid on pot and set in the oven for 3 1/2 to 4 hours. They are done when the meat is falling off the bone.
9. After the Dutch oven has sufficiently cooled, place in refrigerator overnight. The next day, when you're ready to serve, skim the solidified fat from the top with a spoon or by hand with a disposable glove, which is easy to do because it comes off in chunks. This step sounds gross, but it is very important to do before reheating; otherwise, the sauce will be incredibly oily.
10. Place Dutch oven on stove top and reheat on medium-high heat for 15 to 20 minutes.
11. Bring water to a boil for the pasta in a separate pot. Once boiling, add 1 tablespoon of salt to flavor the pasta. Add pasta and cook according to package directions.

12. Place cooked pasta on individual plates and top with short ribs and sauce. Give each serving a generous amount of shaved Parmesan and a sprinkling of chopped parsley for an elegant touch.

Recipe Notes

- Short ribs are the larger and meatier beef equivalent to pork spareribs. I have found that short ribs are carried in limited quantities at most grocers. It is best to call ahead and reserve some for the date you need.
- I always add 4 to 5 boneless short ribs to the pot in the event one of the bone-in ribs is smaller or one cooks down significantly. This will ensure that every guest has a good portion of meat.
- In a pinch you can use fettuccine pasta for this dish, but I would highly recommend pappardelle (pronounced pa-par-day-lay). It is a nice wide noodle, which is easy to cut and doesn't have to be twisted on the fork like other pastas. It looks unique (in a good way), so everyone is usually curious about what it is!

DESSERT:
NEW ORLEANS STRAWBERRIES

Serves 8

My favorite dessert is one my mom made throughout my childhood—New Orleans Strawberries. It is a variation of one of the many strawberry desserts originating in Louisiana. In case you didn't know, Louisiana is all about strawberries! Louisianans knighted the strawberry as their state fruit and come out in droves to celebrate its sweetness at the annual Strawberry Festival each April. This recipe for New Orleans Strawberries may seem like an unusual combination—but they're delicious and deliver as a simple, yet sophisticated after-dinner sweet.

Ingredients You'll Need

5 pounds fresh strawberries
1 1/2 cups full-fat sour cream
1 1/2 cups dark brown sugar

Tools You'll Need

    Spoon
    Knife (optional)

How to Make It

1. Wash and dry the strawberries. Hull them if you wish, but I think it's fun to leave the green tops on in case people would like to use them to hold on to while dipping.
2. Individually plate these, by giving each person 6 strawberries and a healthy dollop of sour cream and heaping mound of brown sugar on the side.
3. Place remaining strawberries, sour cream, and brown sugar in separate serving bowls so guests have the option to help themselves to more. People can dip the strawberries in the sour cream and then into the sugar, or however they please! Although it's perfectly fine to use your hands for this dessert, you can also serve with dessert forks if you've got them, or regular ones will work just fine.

CHAPTER 3

A Sweet Story

The sacrifice the good Lord wants
of us is to die to ourselves.

—St. Charles of Sezze

I was nine years old when my friend told me she was "giving up sugar." "Why?" I asked quizzically. "Because it's not good for you," she said in a know-it-all tone. It was as if she had just watched a *Magic School Bus* episode on the evils of sucrose. I politely nodded, all the while thinking that sugar couldn't be *that* bad, and that giving it up sounded like something I would never want to do.

My love for sugar started young. I loved Nutter Butters, Trix yogurt with sprinkles, Dunkaroos, Gushers, and Fruit Roll-Ups, to name a few old favorites. When Lent rolled around I would identify something sugary to give up, but it was smallish and compartmentalized, like "giving up ice cream." This deserves quotation marks because by "giving up ice cream" I would pivot to some other form of sugar to get my fix.

Over the years, my affinity for all things saccharine continued, although the forms in which it was consumed may have grown a tad more sophisticated. Instead of a pack of frosted animal crackers, it was a hazelnut latte, or at the very least an Americano with one raw sugar. And chocolate. Yes, it's safe to say I had never met a chocolate anything I didn't like.

Then, one fateful summer, my brother Brendan proposed that our family take part in a fast that had three main rules. The first was eating according to traditional fasting rules (two small meals and one modest-sized meal, with no food in between). My inner dialogue: *Okay, I can get behind that.*

25

What's next? The second part included fasting from media and Internet, which meant nothing beyond books and audio books, aside from necessary Internet usage. *Hmmm. I have a few blogs I love visiting, and I've been known to enjoy a good online shopping spree. That's a tough one.* The third part was giving up . . . You guessed it. Sugar. *Hmmmmmm.*

Slowly but surely, every family member, which included ten people (golden retrievers exempt), consented to this wild reform, which was going to last the duration of two Lents. Yes, you read that right—eighty days! Cut to Day 1. I was seriously going through withdrawal. This sounds sad. And that's because it is. The funny thing is, although I loved sugar I would never have said that I had a dependence on sugar. However, after getting a headache that I only ever experienced after going off caffeine during pregnancy, I realized that sugar was a bit of a crutch. I can barely stand to share it, but by Day 2 I was pulling into the Starbucks drive-thru, ordering a grande Americano with—yes—one raw sugar. I'm not proud of it, and I did admit it to my fellow fasters.

The next weeks were pretty grueling because I realized just how much I turned to sugar to get through my day. But as I denied myself those hits of sweet every time I was tempted, I found myself wishing for that piece of chocolate less and less. I had a similar experience with going off the Internet; giving it up made me realize how often I picked up my phone to visit whatever site, without even thinking. I actually went to a favorite blog twice in the beginning before it registered with my brain that I was breaking the rules! It made me aware that anything at your fingertips—that you do not put limits on—can be abused.

I would liken this Lenten-esque crucible—I mean, journey—to looking into a cosmetic mirror, with the special lights and magnification so you can see every fine line you'd rather not notice. This fast was like looking into that mirror. I quickly saw a reflection of the weaker side of my will. And yet, in the discomfort of this self-examination, I was able to improve and grow stronger in ways I would not have otherwise.

As the days wore on, I was surprised to find that my initial feeling of deprivation was replaced by satisfaction. In stripping so much away, I became more content. How was this possible? I reflected on the challenges of the fast. On the food front, fasting sharpened my appetite and I appreciated my food more when I ate. I thought I would be tempted to eat more, but in fact, I had never been so happy with less. I found that abstaining from that insulin spike (and all forms of media, which are mental insulin spikes in their own right) made me turn to more substantial energy sources. Whether it was turning to the Rosary, reading scripture or another book, or working on something on my productivity list, I found that I didn't have the energy crash that I used to have after eating something sugary or wasting minutes on media. On a relationship level, my husband and I felt a deeper satisfaction with how we connected. Not having media demanded more of us. We discovered it's a myth that watching TV together is a connective experience. It really doesn't compare to conversation, walks, going for a drive, or flexing mind-muscles while reading a book together and discussing it along the way. Intensifying quality time raised our game and took our relationship to a new level.

In dwelling on *satisfaction*, I was struck by the word's secondary definition, which is somewhat spiritually attuned: "reparation or compensation for a wrong done or received."[1] In Catholic theology, satisfaction refers to Christ's atonement for sin. St. Thomas Aquinas referred to this as the "repairing of human nature."[2] Christ's suffering, death, and resurrection made reparation for our sin, redeeming (or repairing) our fallen human nature so we could reach a state of grace. I imagine that the bridge between God and man was burned in the Garden of Eden after the original sin, and then many generations later, Christ lay the Cross over the chasm to allow humanity to reconnect with their Creator. This connection with God is available to each of us if we go by way of the Cross. We embrace the Cross in a myriad of ways: by practicing the laws of the Church, having an active prayer life, loving our neighbor, and even doing things like fasting. These are ways of connecting with the Cross because they are often difficult and entail sacrifice, serving as a form of mortification, of dying to oneself. When I participated in the family fast, I reconnected myself to the Cross, and in doing so, I experienced a repairing of my own fallen human nature through the power of Christ.

After the fast was over, my husband asked me, "Do you know what we missed in giving all those things up?" "No, what?" I responded. He said, "Absolutely nothing." I couldn't have agreed with him more. In giving up, we gained. We came to appreciate the little things that before we had taken for granted. Now when I have a piece of chocolate (which is much more rarely these days!), I savor it. After talking with my parents and siblings, I found they had similar experiences. We all were thankful to have gone through it as a group, too, because we supported each other. We prayed together and for one another. We were honest about how hard it was. This was especially beautiful because we were spread out across the country, so it gathered our hearts together in the same spiritual state, and that ended up being the sweetest thing of all.

Prayer for Gathering

"Be Satisfied with Me" is attributed to St. Anthony of Padua.

I want you to stop planning, to stop wishing, and allow Me to give you
The most thrilling plan existing . . . one you cannot imagine.
I want you to have the best. Please allow Me to bring it to you.
You just keep watching Me, expecting the greatest things.
Keep experiencing the satisfaction that I am.
Keep listening and learning the things that I tell you.
Just wait, that's all. Don't be anxious, don't worry.
Don't look around at things others have gotten
Or that I have given them.
Don't look around at the things you think you want.
Just keep looking off and away up to Me,
Or you'll miss what I want to show you . . .
And to enjoy materially and concretely the everlasting union of beauty, perfection, and love that I offer you with Myself.
Know that I love you utterly. I AM God.
Believe it and be satisfied. Amen.

Conclude by saying the Our Father.

Prompts for Conversation

- Have you ever fasted from something? What was your experience like?
- What benefits do you see in the practice of fasting?
- Is there something you can think of that would benefit you to fast from?

Menu: Taco Night

During Lent, when fish fries are so often at the forefront of our Friday nights, it's fair to say that shrimp could use a little love! So, make these spicy shrimp tacos with Sriracha crema the pièce de résistance for your next gathering. The spicy shrimp is balanced by the cooling citrus slaw, and the homemade guac is always a big hit. To finish the meal is a dessert that is as easy as it is fun, Mexican "Fried" Ice Cream (spoiler alert: no frying required). License to yum.

Starter: Guacamole with Grilled Corn and Cotija
Main: Spicy Shrimp Tacos with Sriracha Crema
Side: Citrus Slaw
Dessert: Mexican "Fried" Ice Cream with Homemade Hot Fudge

STARTER:
GUACAMOLE WITH
GRILLED CORN AND COTIJA

Serves 8 (You can use extra guac left over to garnish the tacos.)

Ingredients You'll Need

1 tablespoon olive oil
1 (15.5-ounce) can corn, drained
1/4 teaspoon chili powder
6 avocados, diced
3 small tomatoes, diced
1/3 cup red onion, diced
2 cloves garlic, minced or pressed
2 tablespoons fresh jalapeño, diced
1 lime, juiced

1/2 teaspoon sea salt
1/2 teaspoon cumin
1/4 cup Cotija cheese
Tortilla chips

Tools You'll Need

Measuring spoons
Measuring cups
Skillet
Can opener
Serving bowl
Knife
Spoon

How to Make It

1. Heat a tablespoon of olive oil in a skillet on medium-high heat until it shimmers. Drain the excess liquid from the canned corn and add the corn to the skillet, stirring occasionally for around 10 minutes or until corn starts to brown. It's okay if it gets a little charred because that is the effect you're going for. Once corn is done, stir in the chili powder. Set aside.
2. Dice the avocados. A handy trick is to split the avocado in half, remove the pit, slice the avocado flesh while still inside the skin, and then turn the skin inside out or scoop out the flesh with a spoon.
3. In the bowl that you plan to serve the guac, add all the ingredients and stir gently until combined. Taste to see if it needs more lime juice or salt. Serve with tortilla chips as an appetizer, and then repurpose the guac to garnish the tacos when you're ready to serve.

MAIN:
SPICY SHRIMP TACOS WITH
SRIRACHA CREMA

Serves 8

Ingredients You'll Need

For the Shrimp

    1 pound medium shrimp (about 40 shrimp), fresh or frozen
    1 clove garlic, minced or pressed
    1 teaspoon cumin
    1 teaspoon chili powder
    1/4 teaspoon red pepper flakes
    1/2 teaspoon sea salt
    2 tablespoons olive oil, divided
    2 tablespoons lime juice
    Flour tortillas, large

For the Sriracha Crema

    1 cup sour cream
    4 tablespoons Sriracha

Tools You'll Need

    Colander
    Knife (optional)
    Cutting board (optional)
    Garlic press (optional)
    Citrus juicer
    Large mixing bowl
    Measuring cups
    Measuring spoons
    Small mixing bowl
    Skillet
    Spatula or tongs
    Resealable plastic bag

How to Make It

1. For the shrimp, if you need to defrost, do so according to package instructions.
2. Place defrosted or fresh shrimp in a large mixing bowl, and add all the spices, along with 1 tablespoon of the olive oil and all the lime juice. Toss to coat, and set aside to marinate while you prep the crema. You will also have time to make the Citrus Slaw side (recipe and instructions below).
3. For the crema, in a small serving bowl combine the sour cream and Sriracha. Adjust Sriracha to taste for more or less spice. Spoon crema into a plastic bag and cut the tip off one of the corners, so you can make swirls of crema on the tacos for a nice finishing touch.
4. Now, back to the shrimp: heat the remaining tablespoon of olive oil in a large pan over medium-high heat until it shimmers.
5. Add shrimp to the pan and cook for 4–5 minutes, turning halfway through cooking. Shrimp should turn pink when cooked through. When finished cooking, remove from heat.
6. To build a taco, start with the tortilla, layer with slaw, and top with 5 shrimp. For garnish, add a dollop of guac, crumbled Cotija cheese, and swirls of Sriracha crema.

SIDE:
CITRUS SLAW

Serves 8

Ingredients You'll Need

2 (10-ounce) bags premade coleslaw
1/2 cup extra virgin olive oil
2/3 cup orange juice, freshly
    squeezed (2 oranges)
2 tablespoons cider vinegar
4 teaspoons honey
1 teaspoon sea salt
3 fresh jalapeños, sliced

Tools You'll Need

Large salad bowl
Measuring cups
Measuring spoons
Whisk
Knife
Cutting board

How to Make It

1. Whisk all the dressing ingredients (oil, juice, vinegar, honey, salt) in a large bowl until combined. I always use the bowl I am planning to serve the salad in to cut down on dishes later.
2. Slice fresh jalapeños. Deseed if you (or your guests) prefer less spice.
3. Add the slaw and jalapeño slices to the dressing right before serving. Toss to coat.

DESSERT: MEXICAN "FRIED" ICE CREAM WITH HOMEMADE HOT FUDGE

Serves 8

Ingredients You'll Need

1 quart of vanilla ice cream
8 tablespoons granulated sugar
2 teaspoons ground cinnamon

For "Fried" Coating

6 cups cornflakes, crushed
1 heaping teaspoon ground cinnamon
2 tablespoons butter

For Hot Fudge

1 cup granulated sugar
1 cup unsweetened cocoa powder
1 cup heavy cream or half-and-half

1/2 cup salted butter
2 teaspoons vanilla extract

Toppings

Whipped cream
Cherries
Flaky sea salt, such as Maldon

Tools You'll Need

Baking sheet
Aluminum foil
Measuring cups
Measuring spoons
Resealable plastic bag (gallon)
Rolling pin (optional)
Skillet
Large ice cream scoop
Small mixing bowl
Disposable gloves (optional)
Saucepan
Whisk

How to Make It

1. Line a baking sheet with foil and set aside.
2. Take the ice cream out of the freezer and place on the counter to soften for 20 minutes.
3. While ice cream is softening, pour the cornflakes into a large resealable plastic bag and crush them with a rolling pin or your hands. Once crushed, mix in 1 heaping teaspoon cinnamon.
4. Heat the butter in a skillet over medium heat and add the crushed cinnamon cornflakes. Sauté until the cornflakes are toasted, about 5 minutes.
5. In a small bowl mix together the sugar and remaining cinnamon.
6. When the ice cream is soft enough to form into balls (the size of a large ice cream scoop), make as many as there will be guests.
7. Place the ice cream rounds on the prepared baking sheet and put in the freezer for a *minimum* of 30 minutes.

8. Meanwhile, make the hot fudge. Add the sugar, cocoa powder, and cream to a saucepan and turn to medium heat. Whisk continually until smooth. Once smooth and the pan is warm, add the butter and stir until melted. Remove from heat and add the vanilla. The hot fudge is ready to serve immediately.

9. When ready to serve, take the prepped ice cream from the freezer, roll the rounds in the cinnamon-sugar mixture, and then coat with the toasted cornflakes. A helpful tip is to use disposable gloves for this task so your fingers don't get covered in ice cream and also more easily melt the ice cream. Serve immediately in bowls or on plates (either works!). You can do whatever you want with the whipped cream; make a swirl around the base of the ice cream scoop or make dots around the base and then a swirl on top. Then add hot fudge and a cherry, and maybe a sprinkle of flaky sea salt. Fun and done.

Recipe Notes

- If you make the hot fudge sauce ahead, it keeps in the fridge for a week. When ready to reheat, place in a microwave-safe dish and reheat 30 seconds.
- If someone prefers dairy-free, it's easy to find a dairy-free ice cream and also dairy-free whipped cream so they can enjoy the dessert too.
- A nice finishing touch for each portion is to add a pinch of large flaky sea salt, such as Maldon. It adds a nice twist to have a salty contrast to all the sweet flavors.

CHAPTER 4

Pioneers

Resurgam
I shall rise again.

They say that everything that goes up must come down.

I had just gotten engaged, which was the best of times. This "up," however, was tempered by a shift of another kind: the uncertainty of whether we would stay in the place I had come to call home—Los Angeles.

Going west is in my blood. I was named for a pioneer woman on my mother's side, Catherine Wiley. She and her husband, Elias, lived in Mineral Point, Wisconsin, with their three children. In 1849, when gold fever swept the nation, Elias headed to California. Upwards of three hundred thousand treasure hunters sought riches but left empty-handed, if they left at all. Elias was one of the lucky ones who struck gold—a $50,000 claim, which today would be over $1.5 million. Elias and Catherine took half the gold and invested it in purebred cattle, and then set out with their family on the Oregon Trail.

To make a long story short, Elias died of yellow fever on the journey, which left Catherine responsible for moving the wagon train onward. This was no easy task, and to make matters worse, one evening the cattle got loose in the woods. Due to various dangers, Catherine found no help from the men in rounding the cattle up, so she had to do it herself. It took her until daybreak, and she returned to the camp, only to find her three children abandoned by the wagon train. When Catherine caught up with the group, they were about to cross a big river, which would seal their return home. The story goes that she stood up on her wagon, cocked her rifle, and said,

"I'll shoot the first man to set foot in that river." As you might guess, no one set foot in the river! In the end, Catherine brought her children, her fortune, and the group she was entrusted with safely to Oregon. She went on to be instrumental in founding the Catholic community in Portland. It was known that anyone who needed help could turn to Catherine Wiley, and she would give them a hand.

I heard this story often when I was growing up and found it downright inspiring. Without a doubt it influenced my desire to go west. I wanted to model the grit and guts of this woman, and I always likened setting out to work in the film industry to the Gold Rush, because the odds are about the same—it's called the Boulevard of Broken Dreams for a reason. And yet, I was one of the lucky ones blessed enough to realize my dreams through hard work. I had been a production executive for a Hollywood production company that was Christian-minded and full of good people. I loved what I did, and I wrote and produced a documentary feature film by my late twenties. I was humbled to have such opportunities. But now I was starting a new chapter, and it was one that I was not writing alone.

My soon-to-be-husband, Bryan, and I had talked about the logistics of staying in Southern California since we first met. We both adored the area for many reasons: the perfect weather, gorgeous views, access to so many cool cities, the overall freedom the whole Golden State vibe afforded—and did I mention the beach? Yes, there was plenty to love about SoCal, but there were also drawbacks, and those had to be considered in earnest.

I vividly remember when we started seriously discussing what our future elsewhere could look like. We were en route to a performance of *The Sound of Music* that was playing downtown (yes, my husband is a very good sport), and we started to go back and forth about what life would be like elsewhere. Over time, this discussion transfigured into discernment. Months passed and we got engaged. We started praying a novena to St. Thérèse the Little Flower (who has always been a great intercessor for my family). Even though I was praying for God's will to be revealed, another little part of me was wrapped up in making things come together so that it would seem as if things were too good to leave. In an ideal world, the perfect project would fall into place. And that is exactly what happened. I was asked to cowrite a documentary feature script on the life of Mother Teresa that was going to use exclusive, never-before-seen footage of her life's work in Calcutta, and it would release before her canonization. I was beyond thrilled! Things were going exactly according to my plan—until the unexpected happened. The entire project fell through.

It was a major letdown. It's not as if everything hinged on this project, but it forced me to take a step back. Instead of being so focused on my feelings, which were being fueled by anxiety, I saw that I needed to seek God's heart. That was overwhelming in a lot of ways. And there was bitterness in the thought of leaving the place I had come to know and love. I went to my favorite outdoor workout spot, famously called the "Santa Monica Stairs," which are concrete steps that go up a big hillside with a view of the Pacific Ocean, and I started climbing to clear my mind. Questions whirred through my mind: *Had I done everything I could have professionally? Did I live the LA life to the fullest? What will my friends think? What would life be like somewhere new?* I finished my sets and stood at the top landing to catch my breath. The sunset was glimmering that orange California glow, and the fragrant jasmine filled the air around me. I felt peaceful. I knew I had done my best to make every day count, and my heart felt full.

It was early Easter morning, and Bryan and I were on our way to the Malibu beach. As per our tradition, we would meet up when it was still dark outside, grab coffees from our favorite spot, and drive down the Pacific Coast Highway to the beach, just in time to settle into our beach chairs with blankets to watch the first rays of light burst through the clouds. It was pretty idyllic as the waves crashed against the coast. We kicked off our Easter celebration with homemade orange zest scones, and we both confessed the mutual feeling that our time in California was drawing to a close.

It was fitting that this happened on Easter, because I've always had a special love for the holiday, and things that symbolize Christ's resurrection. For instance, a peacock is a symbol of the Resurrection because it goes through a time of humiliation when it loses all its feathers and looks ugly to the point of hiding for days, but when the peacock reemerges, his feathers are restored and are more vibrant and magnificent than ever. I appreciate how this analogy applies to Christ's death and resurrection, and how it also can apply to our lives. We have mini-deaths with our disappointments, sufferings, and changes, and yet when we discern God's will through it all, we rise and find ourselves better than we were before. This is how it was for me in that time of discernment. I realized this decision about moving was part of discerning my vocation as well. Although it wasn't as natural as knowing that I was called to marriage, and that he was "the one," it brought me to understand what would be best for us, and what would make us thrive as a newly married couple.

A few months later, we did leave California. We caravanned cross-country (which wouldn't have been complete without a car breakdown in the 115-degree Arizona heat!). After a stopover in Kansas City to see my family, we made it to North Carolina. It was a coast-to-coast journey, clocking in at nearly 2,500 miles. After the move, we had many confirmations that our decision was the right one as our lives moved forward in fruitful ways. I came to understand that our journey eastward was pioneering. What defined pioneers was the ability to imagine a different life ahead, regardless of the direction they were headed.

To discern is to pioneer. You have to find your heading by listening to what God wants for your life. It is then that you discover new horizons that lead you to become the person you are called to be.

Prayer for Gathering

By St. Teresa of Avila

> Let nothing disturb thee.
> Let nothing frighten thee.
> All things pass away.
> God never changes.
> Patience attains all things.
> He who has God lacks nothing.
> God alone suffices. Amen.

Conclude by saying the Our Father.

Prompts for Conversation

- When have you experienced a time of discernment?
- Was it expected? Was it difficult? Is it still in process?
- Is there an area of your life where God is currently calling you to discernment?

Menu:
Holiday Brunch

There's nothing quite like a holiday brunch, no matter what occasion you're celebrating. My sisters and I prepared this menu for our Christmas visitors recently to give my mom a break from all the cooking (at least for one meal!). The Bloody Marys keep hungry guests at bay while you prepare the curried avocado toast, the likes of which you would order out. The main is a frittata, which is a complete breakfast baked into one glorious dish, and last but not least are the sweet Hot Cross Buns. You'll have happy guests when you make this meal!

Starter: Bloody Mary Pitcher
Main: Frittata
Side: Curried Avocado Toast
Dessert: Hot Cross Buns

STARTER:
BLOODY MARY PITCHER

Serves 8
Bloody Marys and brunch go hand in hand. This recipe can be thrown together in a flash (and may be consumed even faster). It is the perfect blend of spicy and salty, and even stands on its own with no alcohol added (you can call that version a Bloody Shame).

Ingredients You'll Need

8 tablespoons celery salt (available at your local grocery store)
4 teaspoons lemon pepper or black pepper, freshly ground
2 tablespoons prepared horseradish (This is usually in the refrigerated section but can be difficult to find, so you might ask a grocery store employee for help. It is not the kind you find in the condiment aisle that is already mixed with mayonnaise.)

8 tablespoons Worcestershire sauce
4 tablespoons Tabasco or hot sauce equivalent
4 tablespoons dry sherry (optional) (This is just about 2 ounces.)
1 lemon, juiced
8 cups tomato juice, chilled
1 cup vodka, gin, or tequila
Ice

Optional Garnishes
Celery, washed and cut in long stalks
Bacon strips, cooked
Large olives, pitted
Cherry peppers, jarred
Cornichon pickles
Extra sharp white cheddar cheese, cubed

Tools You'll Need
Large pitcher
Citrus juicer
Skillet
Tongs
Plate lined with paper towels
Measuring spoons
Whisk
Large spoon to stir pitcher
Long toothpicks

How to Make It

1. If you'd like to offer garnishes, prepare and arrange them in advance following steps 2 and 3.
2. Fry bacon on medium-high heat for around 8–10 minutes, flipping to brown each side. When the bacon is cooked through and no pink remains, remove slices to a plate lined with a paper towel, and pat to absorb excess grease.
3. Take a piece of bacon and align it with a celery stick. Now take a toothpick and insert through both celery and bacon to join them together at the top. Add other garnishes to both sides of the toothpick; large olives,

cherry peppers, cornichon pickles, or a cube of extra sharp cheese are a few ideas. Repeat with the rest of the bacon and celery.

4. Take a large pitcher and whisk together the first 7 ingredients, holding back tomato juice and the cup of alcohol.
5. When ready to serve, fill individual glasses with ice.
6. Mix tomato juice and alcohol of choice with pitcher ingredients. Stir thoroughly to evenly distribute the alcohol.
7. After you pour each glass, stir pitcher once again to keep the ingredients easily distributed for each serving. Garnish each glass with prepared celery sticks if you made them. Enjoy!

MAIN: FRITTATA

Serves 8

Ingredients You'll Need

> 2 tablespoons butter to grease the pie plates
> 1 (7-ounce) pack fresh mushrooms, halved
> 16 cherry tomatoes, halved
> 12 bacon slices
> 1 pound sweet or hot Italian sausages, casing removed
> 1 cup (4 ounces) sharp cheddar cheese, grated
> 16 large eggs
> 1/2 cup half-and-half
> 1/2 teaspoon onion powder
> 1/4 teaspoon garlic powder
> 1/4 teaspoon sea salt
> 1/8 teaspoon black pepper, freshly ground

Optional Condiments
> Ketchup
> Grainy mustard
> Hot sauce

Tools You'll Need

    2 (9-inch) pie plates
    Large skillet
    Tongs
    Heatproof spoon or meat turner
    Cheese grater (optional)
    Knife
    Cutting board
    Whisk
    Large mixing bowl
    Measuring cups
    Measuring spoons

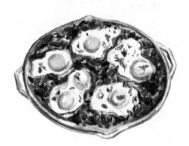

How to Make It

1. Preheat oven to 350 degrees Fahrenheit.
2. Butter two 9-inch pie plates and set aside.
3. Cut mushrooms and tomatoes in half. Set aside.
4. In a large skillet, fry bacon on medium-high heat for around 10 minutes, turning to brown each side. When the bacon is cooked through, remove to a plate lined with a paper towel, and pat to absorb excess grease.
5. Drain bacon grease from the skillet into a heat-safe dish, leaving a coating on the pan for cooking the sausage. (A friendly reminder never to pour grease down your drain as it will harden and clog the drain.) Add sausage to the skillet and brown until no pink remains, for 8–10 minutes. Remove cooked sausage to a plate, leaving the excess grease in the pan.
6. Add mushrooms and cook for 5 to 7 minutes.
7. Add cherry tomatoes and cook 1 more minute.
8. Grate the cheese if not preshredded.
9. Chop the bacon into bite-sized pieces.
10. In a large mixing bowl, whisk eggs and half-and-half, and season with onion powder, garlic powder, salt, and pepper.
11. Add the prepared bacon, sausage, veggies, and half the cheese to the egg mixture. Evenly divide mixture into the prepared pie dishes.
12. Scatter the second half of the cheese over each frittata.
13. Place frittatas in the oven for 30–35 minutes, until set.

14. Cool 5 minutes and cut in fourths to serve. Serve with condiments such as ketchup, mustard, or hot sauce.

Recipe Notes

• Make ahead: You may prepare this ahead (up to 2 hours in advance) by completing all the steps aside from adding the meat and veggie mixture to the eggs. Store all elements in the refrigerator until ready to assemble and cook.
• I find buying cheese by the block and grating it tastes much fresher than preshredded cheese, but either works well.
• Do not over-season with salt, as the bacon and cheese will add salt to the dish too.

SIDE:
CURRIED AVOCADO TOAST

Serves 8

Many decades from now when we think back on this era, we will no doubt remember avocado toast. Delicious and usually totally overpriced when eating out, here is your very own restaurant-grade version to serve to your friends!

Ingredients You'll Need

2 lemons, juiced
6 avocados
1/4 teaspoon sea salt
1/4 teaspoon black pepper, freshly ground, plus more for garnish
3 teaspoons curry powder
6 tablespoons extra virgin olive oil
8 slices sourdough bread

Optional Garnishes
4 radishes, thinly sliced
Flaky sea salt, such as Maldon

Tools You'll Need

Cutting board
Knife
Citrus juicer
Spoon
Measuring spoons
Medium mixing bowl
Small mixing bowl
Toaster
Butter knife

How to Make It

1. If you wish to have radish for garnish, wash and finely slice radishes into paper-thin rounds. Set aside.
2. Juice lemons into a medium mixing bowl. Pit avocados and mash flesh with lemon juice, salt, and pepper. Taste, and add more salt or pepper if you wish.
3. In a small mixing bowl, mix curry powder and extra virgin olive oil. This mixture will have a liquid consistency. Stir into the avocado mixture.
4. Toast the sourdough bread.
5. Generously spread the toast with avocado topping.
6. Add a few radish slivers to the top of each piece for garnish.
7. Give each a final grind of pepper with a pinch of flaky sea salt, and serve!

DESSERT:
HOT CROSS BUNS

Serves 8

Time Note: 3 hours from start to finish

This is my family recipe for hot cross buns. My mother made these for our family every year on Good Friday to enjoy on Easter. Now, I carry on the tradition with my family, and the smell of these freshly baked buns never fails to take me back to those happy Holy Weeks of childhood. Although traditionally baked on Good Friday in honor of Christ's death on the Cross (hence the hot "cross" bun moniker), you can make these anytime. They are the perfect brunch accent, or they can serve as a mean dinner roll. Admittedly, these are a ton of work—but, wow, do these buns deliver. Everyone always appreciates how delicious they are!

Ingredients You'll Need

1/2 cup butter, melted, plus 2 tablespoons for greasing the bowl
1 orange, zested
4 1/2 cups all-purpose flour, plus a teaspoon for dusting
1 packet dry yeast
3/4 cup whole milk
1/3 cup granulated sugar
1/2 teaspoon sea salt
3 eggs
2/3 cup dried blueberries
3/4 teaspoon ground cinnamon
1/4 teaspoon ground nutmeg
Pinch of ground cloves

For the Egg Wash

1 beaten egg white
1 tablespoon water, milk, or cream

For the Frosting

1/2 cup butter, softened
3 cups powdered sugar
Pinch of sea salt
1/2 teaspoon vanilla
4 tablespoons water, milk, or cream to thin frosting

Tools You'll Need

2 large mixing bowls
Zester
Measuring cups
Measuring spoons
Saucepan
Handheld or stand mixer

Wooden spoon
Clean tea towel
Baking sheet
Parchment paper
Knife
Pastry brush (optional)
Wire cooling rack
Frosting gun, frosting bag with tip, or resealable plastic bag

How to Make It

1. Heat oven to 175 degrees Fahrenheit.
2. Grease a large mixing bowl with butter and set aside.
3. Wash and zest the orange. Set the zested orange peel aside.
4. In a large mixing bowl, combine 2 cups of flour and yeast. Set aside.
5. In a saucepan, melt the butter. Add the milk, sugar, and salt and stir with wooden spoon until it is warm to the touch.
6. Add the milk mixture into the bowl of dry ingredients.
7. Add in the eggs and mix for 30 seconds to combine. Scrape the bowl and then beat with a handheld mixer or stand mixer at a high speed for 3 minutes.
8. Next—by hand, using a wooden spoon—stir in the remaining 2 to 2 1/2 cups of flour to form a soft dough. You may not need the last half cup of flour if the dough is coming together well. Stir until just combined.
9. Incorporate the zested orange peel, blueberries, cinnamon, nutmeg, and pinch of cloves.
10. Dust a teaspoon of flour on your hands to keep the dough from sticking, and shape dough into a ball. Place the ball of dough into the prepared mixing bowl, turning over once to coat in the butter.
11. Cover the bowl with a tea towel and set on top of the oven, which should now be warm from preheating to 175 degrees. Turn oven off and allow dough to rest for 1 1/2 hours. The dough will double in size during this time.
12. While you're waiting for the dough to rise, place a piece of parchment paper on a baking sheet for later. (Also, now is a great time to start doing the dishes that have accumulated!)
13. After the dough has risen, punch it down, cover, and allow it to rest for 10 more minutes.

14. Dust flour on your hands again and divide the dough into 8 pieces, forming each into a round the size of a golf ball. You can do this by tearing chunks off the big ball of dough; you do not need to roll it out.

15. Place the dough balls onto the prepared baking sheet, spaced out at least 1 1/2 inches apart.

16. Cover and allow to rise for 35 minutes. The buns will double in size again during this time.

17. Preheat the oven to 375 degrees.

18. While waiting on the buns to rise, make your egg wash: mix up the egg white and tablespoon of water, milk, or cream with a whisk or a fork.

19. When the buns have risen, take a sharp knife and cut a cross shape on top of each bun—not deep enough to slice the roll into quarters, but enough to leave an impression. As per tradition, you can bless each bun as you go: "In the name of the Father, and of the Son, and of the Holy Spirit."

20. Brush the prepared egg wash over the buns with a pastry brush if you have one, and if not, you can go the old-fashioned route and use your fingers.

21. Place the buns in the 375-degree oven and bake for 12–15 minutes (until golden brown).

22. Remove buns from oven and place them on a cooling rack. Allow them to cool completely before frosting.

23. As the buns cool, mix up the frosting. Using a handheld mixer or stand mixer, beat the butter and add in the powdered sugar, salt, vanilla, and the water, milk, or cream until thick frosting forms.

24. To frost you can use a frosting gun or a frosting bag with tip (both available at local craft stores), or you can scoop the frosting into a resealable plastic bag and cut the edge off to make a frosting bag. (This is the technique used in the earlier recipe for cannoli cups.)

25. Make a large cross on each of the buns with the frosting. Allow the frosting to set at least 30 minutes and then gently cover with wax paper for freshness. Do not stack these, because it will smoosh the frosting!

Recipe Notes

- Make ahead: These hot cross buns can be made a day in advance and lightly covered with plastic wrap. Do not put in a sealed container, as it will cause them to moisten.
- Read the recipe before you begin as there are so many steps!

CHAPTER 5

Closer to Eden

Time began in a garden.

As a child I always liked to imagine the Garden of Eden. All leafy and lush, with flora and fauna coexisting in harmony—the thought of it still makes my heart swoon. Despite my love of Eden, I've never been much of a green thumb. Through my apartment-dwelling years, I purchased more plants than I would like to admit that met withered ends—all of which I usually blamed on an obvious microclimate effect or a plant being "temperamental." As I've grown older (and a little wiser) I've learned faux is the way to go. No maintenance was my salvation! So imagine my dismay when, after moving into my first house, I discovered that the live plants (and weeds) outside needed a whole lot of tending to.

When my husband and I moved into our house, the yard was in good shape, to the point where I didn't even give it much thought. Before we knew it two summers blazed by, and on one muggy morning I found myself, coffee in hand, peering outside—not into a backyard—but into a jungle. To paint you a picture, our yard has a perimeter covered in pine straw, which is extremely weed-prone (and when you envision weeds, you need to think medium-tree height). Our yard also has some very bushy areas that seemed better to leave alone because they were, well, bushy. I decided to have some yard-service companies come over and give an estimate as to how we were going to turn this place around.

After many a company came, and all was said and quoted, every estimate rang in upwards of two thousand dollars. Yup. That wasn't happening. My husband and I were not going to spend that kind of money to clear out weeds. So we set to work. But, weeds! How do I loathe thee? Let me count the ways . . . Something about weeding truly drives me insane because every time I pull one up I invariably see one I missed, and even if I get all of them, a few newbies will be cropping up in a matter of days. I stewed in the injustice of it all as I weeded, but as I worked I felt a cool breeze and heard the calming sound of rustling leaves. My thoughts soon turned from gardening fury to wondering if there was a spiritual reason I was doing so much weeding. My mind jumped to the biblical parable of the sower and the idea of hearts being like soil.

Later that night I read the parable in the Gospel of Matthew (13:1–23) where Jesus describes four kinds of hearts who receive the Word of God. First, the seed is sown on the path. This heart does not understand the message of the Christ, and the evil one snatches the seeds away. Second, the seed falls on rocky ground. The message of Christ is received with joy but does not take root. When difficulty arises because of the Word, this heart turns away. Third, the seed falls on thorns. The Word cannot take root because "worldly anxiety" chokes it (verse 22). Fourth, the seed falls on good soil. This heart hears the Word, understands it, and holds to it faithfully. The yield of the seed is thirty, sixty, or even one hundred times what was sown.

The next morning I took to the battlefield of my backyard once more, and while I dug up mounds of weeds, I also unearthed a spiritual analogy comparing the parable to my heart. *Which heart was I?* In the past I had always identified with the fourth heart, but now I wasn't so sure. The previous year had been so busy with a new baby that my prayer life was thrown into a tailspin. I had always loved prayer and had gone to Mass daily whenever I could, but with a baby on board, the old schedules weren't possible for me. It made me realize that I had taken for granted my closeness with God in the past because nothing had competed for it. Even when I worked eighty hours a week, I made time for God, but ever since I had been working around the clock with my sweet baby girl, God had been relegated to the back burner. My heart was being choked by the thorns—or as I'd like to imagine, weeds—namely, the "worldly anxiety" that currently translated to the all-consuming constant care for a child.

As the sun began to beat down, I knew I needed to renew my relationship with God. A quote from St. Augustine floated through my mind: "This very moment I may, if I desire, become the friend of God." I felt encouraged as I knew that rekindling a friendship was totally possible, but it would require cultivation. Yet another weeding analogy sprung up for me: for weeds to be defeated you must pull them from the roots, and that takes more effort than addressing them at a surface level. My weeds of worry and distraction would not be uprooted without going deep. I knew I couldn't simply say, *I will pray every day*. I needed a plan to tend to the garden of my heart.

As I reflected on relationship building, the five love languages came to mind: words of affirmation, quality time, gifts, physical touch, acts of service.[1] Why not apply these to my wilting relationship with our Lord? Words of affirmation would be spending time with his Word every morning before I even got out of bed; quality time would be making a holy hour every week in eucharistic adoration; gifts would be a prayer offering every day, such as the Rosary; physical touch would be more frequent Holy Communion; and acts of service, although my time was stretched thin, would be to volunteer in some small way, even if it meant bringing a ham to an Easter food drive. This was my plan.

After a week, the backyard began to improve. We got things to a place where we could get a new quote that was less than a fourth of the initial estimates, and so we were able to get help trimming trees and hauling away brush. Soon enough, the backyard was a haven. We had friends over who looked into the backyard and asked if a patio structure we had was new. Nope, it had just been obstructed by overgrowth in the past! It's amazing the new life given to a space by intentional work to get it right. The same applied to righting my relationship with God. I saw the intentional cultivation pay off immediately. The time I set aside to reconnect with God on a love-language level, as if I was connecting with a person, made me feel more restored to keep up with my daily routine as a wife and mother, and it even seemed to multiply my time to get stuff done throughout the day. I saw the wisdom in keeping our hearts as a garden should be kept, so that people can see and take delight in it—even if that someone is yourself—and that is what keeps us closer to Eden.

Prayer for Gathering

A classic Catholic prayer

Oh, Jesus, meek and humble of heart, make my heart like unto thine. Amen.

Conclude by saying the Our Father.

Prompts for Conversation

- Are you familiar with the five love languages (words of affirmation, quality time, gifts, physical touch, acts of service)? Which do you rank most important for you?
- Has there been a time when your heart has been in the weeds? How did you get through?
- How do you set aside moments to have quality time with God during the day?

Menu:
Afternoon Tea

An afternoon tea is meant to be a light meal consisting of three courses of tea sandwiches, followed by scones or sweet pastry. I love a good tea, and my sisters, knowing this, prepared this menu for my baby shower. It was absolutely stellar. It's perfect for a garden party, a bridal or baby shower, Mother's Day, or a brunch. Try this menu out for a special gathering!

Starter: Tea
Main: Trio of Tea Sandwiches: Cucumber on White Bread, Curry-Macadamia Chicken Salad on Sweet Brown Bread, and Smoked Salmon Dill Rounds on Rye Bread
Side: Watermelon Fruit Bowl with Lemon Curd Dip
Dessert: Scones with Blackberry Butter

 # STARTER:
TEA

Variety

When selecting tea for your gathering, try at least two types from different flavor palettes. Some classic options are: black teas, such as Earl Grey or English breakfast; herbal teas, such as chamomile or peppermint; and scented oolong teas, such as jasmine or green.

Add-Ins

It is thoughtful to provide sweeteners of sugar and honey for your guests. I like to offer turbinado sugar cubes and honey in a dish with a honey spoon.

It's also a must to offer milk, cream, creamer, or dairy-free milk (depending on dietary restrictions) in a small pitcher.

Serving

The traditional way to serve tea is to steep it in a teapot, but doing that for several varieties of tea can be complicated depending on the size of your group. A simple alternative is to have hot water in several teapots, along with a selection of tea bags or loose-leaf teas arranged for your guests, so they can make their own individual cups.

MAIN:
TRIO OF TEA SANDWICHES

Tea is traditionally served from 3:00 to 5:00 in the afternoon, and at that time it is more of a snack than a meal. It's possible, however, that you will be hosting a brunch or luncheon, where the tea sandwiches will be the main meal. I offered three sandwich varieties because I hope you will find each to be a delicious addition to your recipe repertoire, but they certainly do not need to be made all at once! Depending on the size and type of your gathering, you could make as much or as little of the menu as you wish. The tea sandwiches included on this menu are small and with a serving size of three sandwiches per person, based on a group of eight guests. If you're having a few friends to tea, you could simply make the scones and blackberry butter—whatever suits your needs best!

MAIN SANDWICH ONE:
CUCUMBER ON WHITE BREAD

Serves 8 (amounts to 3 sandwiches per guest)

Ingredients You'll Need

  1 seedless cucumber, grated
  2 teaspoons fresh dill, chopped
  8 ounces plain cream cheese, softened

3 tablespoons mayonnaise
1 dash Worcestershire sauce
1/4 teaspoon garlic powder
1/4 teaspoon onion salt
1 pinch lemon pepper or black pepper, freshly ground
1 loaf of sliced white sandwich bread

Tools You'll Need

Grater
Paper towel
Knife
Cutting board
Measuring spoons
Handheld or stand mixer
Spoon
Butter knife

How to Make It

1. Grate the cucumber. Place the grated cucumber in a paper towel and squeeze the excess water out. You may need to do this a few times with a fresh paper towel, as cucumbers are quite watery. Set aside.
2. Finely chop the dill. Set aside.
3. Using a handheld or stand mixer, blend cream cheese and mayonnaise for 30 seconds or until combined.
4. Stir in the cucumber, chopped dill, Worcestershire sauce, garlic powder, onion salt, and pepper.
5. Cut the crusts off the bread.
6. Spread some of the cream cheese mixture on a bread slice, and top with a bread slice. Repeat with remaining slices and mixture.
7. Cut each sandwich into 3 rectangular pieces.

Recipe Notes

- Make ahead: You can make the filling the day before and store it in an airtight container in the refrigerator.
- If you want to assemble the sandwiches in advance, they can be covered in plastic wrap and stored in the refrigerator up to 24 hours.

MAIN SANDWICH TWO:
CURRY-MACADAMIA CHICKEN SALAD
ON SWEET BROWN BREAD

Adapted from Ina Garten: "Curried Chicken Salad"[2]
Serves 8 (amounts to 3 sandwiches per guest)

Ingredients You'll Need

For Brown Bread

    2 tablespoons butter, for greasing pan
    4 cups whole wheat flour
    1 cup plus 6 tablespoons all-purpose flour
    2 cups brown sugar
    4 teaspoons baking soda
    4 cups buttermilk

For Curry-Macademia Chicken Salad

    6 boneless, skinless chicken breasts
    3 tablespoons olive oil
    Sea salt and freshly ground black pepper, for seasoning
    1 cup red grapes, halved
    1/2 cup green onions, finely chopped
    3 cups mayonnaise
    2/3 cup dry white wine, like a fruity, unoaked Chardonnay (optional)
    1/2 cup mango chutney, or apricot preserves
    6 tablespoons curry powder
    1 teaspoon sea salt
    2 cups salted macadamias, chopped

Tools You'll Need

    2 bread loaf pans (9x5 inch)
    Measuring cups
    Measuring spoons
    Medium mixing bowl
    Sifter (optional)
    Wooden spoon
    Butter knife

Knife
Cutting board
Baking sheet
Aluminum foil
Meat thermometer
Mixing bowl
Whisk
Resealable bag or container

How to Make It

1. Preheat oven to 350 degrees Fahrenheit.
2. Grease loaf pans with butter. (As this recipe will make two loaves, remember to cut ingredients in half if you only need one.)
3. In a medium mixing bowl, sift or combine dry ingredients with a wooden spoon.
4. Stir in buttermilk until thoroughly combined, but do not overmix.
5. Pour batter into loaf pans and bake for 45 minutes. Remove from oven and insert a knife to test that it's baked. If the knife does not come out clean, then place in oven for 5 more minutes and test again. For easier slicing, cool the bread completely, but if you're enjoying the bread by itself, serve fresh out of the oven. Each loaf should yield 12 slices.
6. For the chicken, prepare baking sheet with foil. Place the chicken breasts on the sheet pan and rub the skin with olive oil and season with salt and pepper.
7. Bake at 350 degrees for 25–30 minutes or until internal temperature reaches 165 degrees.
8. Set chicken aside to cool.
9. While chicken cools, halve the grapes, and finely chop the green onions. When chicken has cooled, dice into small pieces.
10. To make the dressing, whisk the mayonnaise, wine (if using), chutney or preserves, curry powder, and salt in a mixing bowl until smooth.
11. Add prepared chicken, grapes, and green onions to the dressing bowl. Refrigerate chicken salad for at least 2 hours (or up to overnight) so the flavors can meld.
12. Chop macadamias and store in a resealable plastic bag or container for when you are ready to serve.

13. Remove the chicken salad 30 minutes before serving to bring to room temperature, and then add the chopped macadamias.

14. To assemble the sandwiches, slice the bread, and cut the crusts off before cutting them diagonally into triangles. If you cut the bread in pairs of two slices, they will be evenly matched for the sandwiches. As close to the gathering as possible, spread the curried chicken on precut triangles to make the sandwiches. Serve immediately.

Recipe Notes

• If you don't have buttermilk and you're in a pinch, you can make your own. For every cup of buttermilk you need, take a cup of milk and stir in 1 tablespoon lemon juice or use any of the following vinegars: white, rice, or cider. Let it sit for 10 minutes. It should curdle slightly, and then you have homemade buttermilk.

MAIN SANDWICH THREE: SMOKED SALMON DILL ROUNDS ON RYE BREAD

Serves 8 (amounts to 3 sandwiches per guest)

Ingredients You'll Need

2 sticks unsalted butter, room temperature
1/8 teaspoon garlic powder
2 tablespoons green onions, finely chopped
2 tablespoons fresh dill, finely chopped, plus extra for garnish
2 tablespoons parsley, finely chopped
2 teaspoons lemon juice
1 teaspoon sea salt
1/2 teaspoon black pepper, freshly ground
2 loaves of dark grain bread or rye
1 (4-ounce) package of smoked salmon

Tools You'll Need

Handheld or stand mixer
4-inch round cookie cutter (optional)
Glass or teacup (optional)
Knife
Cutting board
Butter knife
Measuring spoons
Citrus juicer (optional)
Kitchen scissors (optional)
Plastic wrap

How to Make It

1. To make the herb butter, use a handheld or stand mixer to combine softened butter with garlic powder, green onions, chopped dill, parsley, lemon juice, salt, and pepper. Beat on low until just combined, around 30 seconds.

2. Lay out the bread slices and cut rounds out of the centers with cookie cutter until you have 24 rounds. You will get one round from each slice. If you do not have a 4-inch cookie cutter, take a glass or teacup with a 4-inch opening; place it over the bread and cut around the edge of the glass with a sharp knife to achieve your round. Save the leftover bread to make breadcrumbs or croutons so as not to waste!

3. Slice the smoked salmon in quadrants to yield 24 pieces.

4. Spread the 24 bread rounds with the herb butter and add a piece of smoked salmon on top of each.

5. With kitchen scissors or a knife, cut sprigs of the leftover fresh dill and add one to the top of each round. Cover in plastic wrap and refrigerate until ready to serve. Best served chilled.

Recipe Notes

• Make ahead: You can make the herb butter 3 days in advance and store in the refrigerator. You can also cut the rounds the day before and store them in an airtight container. This leaves the salmon and dill garnish to be cut at the last minute for quick assembly the morning of the gathering.

- The average loaf of rye yields 24 slices. I suggest buying 2 in the event a loaf is smaller than average. If you don't use the second one, you can freeze it for later use.

SIDE:
WATERMELON FRUIT BOWL
WITH LEMON CURD DIP

Serves 8

Ingredients You'll Need

For Dip

    2 cups (16 ounces) full-fat Greek yogurt, plain or vanilla, or sour cream

    3/4 cup lemon curd

    1–2 tablespoons powdered sugar

    2 teaspoons lemon zest (1 medium lemon), for garnish

For Fruit Bowl

    1 whole large watermelon, seedless

    8 cups seasonal, assorted fruit, such as blueberries, strawberries (hulled and halved), kiwis, nectarines, mangoes, pineapples, seedless grapes, cantaloupe, honeydew melon, or anything you'd like!

    2 tablespoons olive oil (optional)

    8 ounces feta cheese (optional)

Tools You'll Need

    Measuring cups

    Measuring spoons

    Small mixing bowl

    Spoon

    Grater or zester

    Small serving bowl

    Plastic wrap

    Knife

    Cutting board

    Grater

How to Make It

1. Place yogurt or sour cream, lemon curd, and powdered sugar together in a small mixing bowl and combine with a spoon until smooth, about 30 seconds.
2. Remove lemon peel with grater or zester. If you don't have one of these on hand, you can use a vegetable peeler to remove lemon peel and then finely dice it to a zest-like consistency.
3. Place dip in small serving bowl, sprinkle with the lemon zest, and cover and refrigerate for at least 1 hour.
4. To make your fruit bowl, carefully cut a length-wise hole along the top of the watermelon, taking care not to cut too far into the sides of the rind. (If you want to get fancy, you can cut a zigzag pattern around the opening for decorative effect.) Scoop out watermelon flesh and save to add to your fruit bowl; or later you can try grilling it with a drizzling of olive oil until charred on each side, and pair it with fresh feta!
5. Cut the fresh fruit you plan to use into bite-sized pieces.
6. Fill bowl with prepared fruit.
7. Remove dip from fridge when ready to serve with fruit bowl. Best served chilled.

Recipe Notes

• Make ahead: The watermelon bowl can be made the night before, wrapped in plastic wrap, and stored in the refrigerator. The fruit can be prepared a few hours in advance. The dip can be made the day before and stored in the refrigerator.

DESSERT:
SCONES WITH BLACKBERRY BUTTER

Serves 8

I've tried many scone recipes through the years, and this one is by far my favorite. These are a scrumptious treat with the blackberry butter, or they can be the base palette for experimenting with different flavor combinations such as white-chocolate-cherry, maple-pecan, or a savory variation like bacon, cheddar, and chive (see recipe notes).

Ingredients You'll Need

For Scones

> 2 cups all-purpose flour, plus 2 tablespoons for dusting
> 1/3 cup granulated sugar
> 1 tablespoon baking powder
> 1/2 teaspoon salt
> 1/2 cup cold butter, cut into 1/2-inch cubes
> 1 cup heavy cream, plus 4 tablespoons

For Blackberry Butter

> 8 ounces blackberries, fresh
> 1 tablespoon lemon juice (half a lemon, juiced)
> 1/4 cup powdered sugar
> 2 sticks butter, softened

Tools You'll Need

> Baking sheet
> Parchment paper
> Measuring cups
> Measuring spoons
> 2 large mixing bowls
> Sifter (optional)
> Pastry blender or pastry cutter (optional)
> Large spoon
> Knife
> Cutting board
> Pastry brush (optional)

Small saucepan
Citrus juicer (optional)
Small mixing bowl
Handheld or stand mixer

How to Make It

1. Preheat oven to 450 degrees Fahrenheit.
2. Place a sheet of parchment paper on a baking sheet. Set aside.
3. In a large bowl, mix (and sift, if possible) the flour, sugar, baking powder, and salt.
4. Cube the cold butter and then "cut the butter" into the flour mixture with your hands. "Cutting butter" means rubbing the pieces of butter into the flour so that the mixture becomes crumbly. Do not try to beat the butter in, as this will not achieve the desired effect. If you have a pastry blender or pastry cutter, then by all means, use that. I often go the old-fashioned route and use my hands, and it turns out fine.
5. Place mixture in freezer for 5 minutes.
6. Remove mixture from freezer and add 1 cup plus 2 tablespoons of heavy cream and stir with a large spoon until just combined. It should be in a moistened dough-like form at this point. If it is still crumbly, add extra cream in increments of tablespoons until no crumbles remain. You may need to work it in with your hands. The dough will not be perfectly smooth; it may even be in broken sections, but that is okay because you will mold it into a round.
7. Turn the dough out onto a large sheet of parchment paper and dust your hands with flour before you gently press the dough into a 7-inch round, making the edges as clean as possible by pushing them inward.
8. Cut dough into 8 wedges.
9. Place scones on the prepared baking sheet, so they are not touching.
10. Take the remaining 2 tablespoons of cream and brush on the top of scones with a pastry brush, or using your fingers.
11. Bake at 450 degrees Fahrenheit for 12–15 minutes. Watch them as they bake to see if they start to get too golden before they are done. If they are fully golden and still have several minutes to go, quickly remove the baking sheet from the oven and add a sheet of parchment paper over the scones to stop the browning. They should be airy but pretty firm to

the touch when they are done. Serve warm if possible, but if not, they'll still be delicious!

12. For the blackberry butter, in a small saucepan, heat the blackberries on medium heat with lemon juice and powdered sugar for 5 minutes, stirring occasionally and crushing the blackberries as they soften. The blackberries should be roughly broken down by the end but do not need to be perfectly smooth.

13. Transfer mixture out of the warm pan into a small mixing bowl, and allow to cool for at least 15 minutes.

14. Place the sticks of softened butter in a large mixing bowl, and beat using a handheld or stand mixer on a low setting until smooth; then slowly add the blackberry mixture until combined and the butter has blackberry swirls throughout.

15. Serve the scones with the blackberry butter on the side.

Recipe Notes

- Make ahead: The blackberry butter can be made in advance and stored in the refrigerator for up to 4 days. You can also freeze it for a month and thaw the day before your gathering in the refrigerator.

- Here are flavor variations for the scones that you can try:

  * White-Chocolate-Cherry: When adding the cream, stir in 1/3 cup dried cherries (chopped) and 1/4 cup white chocolate chips.

  * Maple-Pecan: Substitute brown sugar for granulated sugar. When adding the cream, stir in 1/2 cup toasted pecans (chopped). If you have it, sprinkle turbinado sugar on the tops of the scones after brushing them with cream. Glaze the scones after they cool with maple glaze. To make the glaze, place 3/4 cup powdered sugar (sifted) in a bowl and add 2 tablespoons heavy cream and 2 teaspoons maple syrup. Stir together until a glaze forms and no powdered sugar clumps remain.

  * Bacon, Cheddar, and Chive: Omit sugar entirely. When adding the cream, stir in 1/2 teaspoon freshly ground pepper, 3/4 cup sharp cheddar (shredded), 1/4 cup cooked bacon (finely chopped), and 2 tablespoons fresh chives (finely chopped).

CHAPTER 6

Peace over Perfect

Perfect is the enemy of the good.

—Aristotle

I have a penchant for perfectionism. Although I could not be categorized as a complete "type A," I am someone who is pretty particular about things being done "right." As my husband once put it, "With you, it's either symphony or silence." I couldn't argue with him. My perfectionistic propensity leads me to take things a bit too seriously at times, and it's been a lifelong process of remembering to lighten up, even when things don't go my way.

One homily helped me frame this process as a quest for finding humor in all situations. The priest asked everyone to think of the crown jewel of the virtues. To my surprise, he gave a virtue that wasn't a cardinal virtue, or a theological virtue; it wasn't one of the fruits of the Spirit either. Instead, he named the crown jewel of all virtues as *humor*. I thought it was a brilliant insight. After all, Mark Twain famously said, "Humor is mankind's greatest blessing."

I do try to have a sense of humor when I find myself pitted against perfectionism. This sense of humor helps me to see a situation in a different light, and ultimately it casts a vision of peace. It was with this mindset that I set about planning my wedding. With caricatures of bridezilla dancing around in my imagination, and often hearing stories of wedding stress preempting marital bliss, I was determined not to fall prey to these pitfalls. I'm happy to say that things went well leading up to the big day. I could imagine a sign above my head—like the type displayed in factories noting how many days since their last accident—only with a modification: 173 days of peace over perfect.

I'm sure part of my success in this had to do with my better half, who has the uncanny ability to retain a peaceful perspective in almost any situation. His even-keel nature serves as the rock of reason when I'm about to spiral into worry over—you name it. For instance, if we don't have sun-dried tomatoes to add to the pasta that already has six other ingredients incorporated, I find it imperative to go to the store and get said sun-dried tomatoes, no matter how inconvenient. My husband, on the other hand? He would vote to omit them.

It was with this level-headed spirit that my husband approached all our wedding planning. He said on numerous occasions that it would be wise to expect at least something big to go wrong and to steel ourselves so as not to let it spoil the day. We were focusing on the Sacrament of Marriage, the witness of our love among loved ones, and that was bigger than quibbling over details that in the end paled in comparison of importance. I was on board with this—until the "something big" actually happened.

Our wedding date was June 24, and the location was my hometown of Kansas City. If you've never been to Kansas City in the summer, then I will tell you what the weather app would read: "95 degrees Fahrenheit, but feels like 108." That summer, temps were registering hotter than those in India, and so it was a bit of a wrinkle when on the eve of our wedding, we got a call. It was from the reception venue. Bad news, they said. The air conditioning was out of order.

Now, I have heard a lot of wedding "hiccup" stories—everything from a bride walking down the aisle sans her veil, a groom fainting at the altar, a cake MIA because of a date mix-up, dress tailoring gone wrong at the last minute, flowers looking dreadful, rain with an outdoor venue. No AC in the sweltering summer heat was going to be right up there with the worst of them, and my track record of tranquility was being put to the test.

As soon as I told my groom about the bad news, he practiced what he preached and reacted with a "keep calm, carry on" attitude. I remember we both laughed (for my part, to keep from crying), but that was the humor element at work. We then said a Hail Mary that it could be resolved and made a pact not to tell a soul that the AC was broken, because then everyone would think it was ten times hotter than it actually was. My dad came up with a solution and insisted that high-quality mobile AC units be brought into the venue. This was done, and they were cleverly disguised behind decorative curtains so they weren't sticking out like sore thumbs.

The morning of our wedding came, and knowing our guests would be celebrating in an air-conditioned venue was a tremendous relief. Before we knew it, we had said our vows and the bells were ringing. A little later, when the reception was in full swing, we were so thankful to hear everyone saying how *cool* it felt. People danced the night away, and then we had our send-off. The song we selected in advance turned out to be very apropos—one that is all about staying positive: "Peace Train" by Cat Stevens.

The merit of peace over perfect on our wedding day is one my husband and I still talk about. It would have been "perfect" to have working AC, but in the end, the venue was as cool, if not cooler, than it would have been. In the heat of the moment, we could have had meltdowns that we would have regretted, but in keeping our sense of humor, we could end the night with no regrets. As "Peace Train" played, the sparklers waved, and our vintage Mustang convertible roared into the night, it was a good feeling to know that our commitment to peace over perfect saved the date.

Prayer for Gathering

Prayer for Good Humor by St. Thomas More

Grant me, O Lord, good digestion, and also something to digest.
Grant me a healthy body, and the necessary good humor to maintain
   it.
Grant me a simple soul that knows to treasure all that is good
and that doesn't frighten easily at the sight of evil,
but rather finds the means to put things back in their place.
Give me a soul that knows not boredom, grumblings, sighs and
   laments,
nor excess of stress, because of that obstructing thing called "I."
Grant me, O Lord, a sense of good humor.

Allow me the grace to be able to take a joke to discover in life a bit
   of joy,
and to be able to share it with others. Amen.

Conclude by saying the Our Father.

Prompts for Conversation

- What do you think about humor being considered the crown jewel of all virtues?
- Have you had a time when humor helped you be more thoughtful or kind?
- What are your thoughts on the following quote from Aristotle? "Perfect is the enemy of the good."

Menu: Salad Day Soiree

This summer luncheon menu is almost as refreshing as a sense of humor. A steak cobb salad with sweet potato fries has been a go-to lunch menu of mine for years, and I have made it for get-togethers more times than I can count. For dessert, the best-ever chocolate chunk cookies live up to their name. Welcome your guests with a refreshment of lemonade iced tea with mint or some rosé sangria. Cheers!

Starter: Lemonade Iced Tea with Mint *or* Rosé Sangria
Main: Steak Cobb Salad
Side: Sweet Potato Fries with Dip
Dessert: Best-Ever Chocolate Chunk Cookies

STARTER:
LEMONADE ICED TEA
WITH MINT OR ROSÉ SANGRIA

LEMONADE ICED TEA

Serves 8

Ingredients You'll Need

   Iced tea
   Lemonade
   Fresh mint leaves, washed

Tools You'll Need

   Pitcher
   Large spoon
   Ice

How to Make It

1. Combine equal parts iced tea and lemonade in a pitcher. I buy both of these premade for simplicity's sake.
2. Fill glasses with ice and sprigs of fresh mint leaves for garnish. Pour right before the gathering begins.

ROSÉ SANGRIA

Serves 8

Ingredients You'll Need

    1 (750-milliliter) bottle dry rosé wine
    1/2 cup cranberry juice (not juice cocktail)
    1/4 cup granulated sugar
    3 tablespoons Cointreau (1.5 ounces)
    1 tablespoon brandy (0.5 ounces)
    1 (16-ounce) container fresh strawberries, hulled and quartered
    1 (6-ounce) container fresh raspberries
    1 liter sparkling water, chilled

Tools You'll Need

    Knife
    Cutting board
    Wine corkscrew
    Measuring spoons
    Measuring cups
    Pitcher
    Large spoon
    Plastic wrap

How to Make It

1. Wash fruit. Hull and quarter strawberries and set aside.
2. In a pitcher, combine the rosé, cranberry juice, sugar, Cointreau, and brandy. Stir with a large spoon until the sugar dissolves, and then add the strawberries and raspberries.

3. Cover and refrigerate for at least 2 hours but ideally overnight.
4. When ready to serve, fill glasses nearly full with sangria and top off with a little sparkling water.
5. Serve right away.

Recipe Notes

- Make ahead: Try making this the night before to let the fruit infuse and flavors meld. If you don't have the time and it's more last minute, go for it on the same day, because it will still taste great!
- If you are serving 8 people, I recommend pouring the wine mixture into all the glasses first and then adding the fruit from the bottom of the pitcher. This will ensure that you don't accidentally over pour and end up short. This serves 8 with none left over!

MAIN:
STEAK COBB SALAD

Serves 8

Ingredients You'll Need

For Dressing
    6 tablespoons olive oil
    4 tablespoons red wine vinegar
    2 tablespoons lemon juice (2 lemons juiced)
    2 heaping teaspoons Dijon mustard
    2 teaspoons Worcestershire sauce
    2 cloves garlic, minced or pressed
    1/2 teaspoon sea salt
    1/2 teaspoon black pepper, freshly ground

For Salad
    Sea salt and freshly ground black pepper, for seasoning
    2 pounds chicken tenders or chicken thighs
    8 eggs, hard-boiled
    10 slices of bacon
    4 steaks, such as rib eye or New York strip

4 tablespoons butter
1/2 pound Black Forest ham, diced
8 medium tomatoes, diced
4 avocados, diced
2 (9-ounce) bags romaine lettuce
1 cup crumbled blue cheese

Tools You'll Need

Sheet pan or baking dish
Aluminum foil
Meat thermometer
Cutting board
Knife
Pot to boil eggs
Slotted spoon
Skillet
Tongs
Measuring cups
Measuring spoons
Whisk
Small pitcher or bowl for dressing
Large salad bowl for serving

How to Make It

1. Preheat oven to 400 degrees Fahrenheit.
2. Line a baking sheet or dish with foil. Season chicken with a sprinkling of salt and pepper and place in prepared dish.
3. When oven is heated, bake chicken for 30–35 minutes or until internal temperature reaches 165 degrees. Allow to cool, and chop into bite-size pieces.
4. While the chicken is in the oven, place eggs in a pot and cover with cold water until just submerged. Bring to a boil and then reduce to simmer and cover for 8 minutes. When done, remove with a slotted spoon and allow to cool while you start the bacon.
5. Heat a large skillet over medium-high heat. Add the bacon slices and cook for 8-10 minutes, turning midway through and removing when no pink remains.

6. While bacon is cooking, slice the steaks into strips and season with salt and pepper.
7. When bacon is cooked, remove to plate covered in a napkin or paper towel (this absorbs the excess grease).
8. Carefully drain bacon grease into a heat-safe dish to discard later. A friendly reminder to be extra careful and to never put grease down the drain because it will harden and clog your drain.
9. Taking the skillet you used for the bacon, heat a tablespoon of butter over medium-high heat and add a fourth of the sliced steak. Brown the steak 1–2 minutes per side. You can cook to preference, but it's advisable not to serve overly well done as that can affect the texture. Repeat with the remaining butter and steak until all is cooked.
10. Chop the bacon into large chunks and set aside.
11. Peel the hard-boiled eggs. A helpful tip is to crack the egg and peel the shell off under running water or in a bowl of water. The shell comes off more easily this way. Chop each egg into fourths and set aside.
12. Chop the ham, tomatoes, and avocado into bite-sized chunks.
13. Whisk together all the ingredients for the dressing and pour into a small pitcher or bowl (this dressing is served on the side).
14. To assemble the salad, start by filling your large salad bowl or platter with the lettuce. Add the toppings in rows: chicken, bacon crumbles, diced avocado, tomato, eggs, steak tips, ham, and cheese. It looks more artful than tossing it all in the bowl and also allows people to get good portions of each topping. Serve with dressing on the side.

Recipe Notes

- Make ahead: This salad can be prepped in advance by making the dressing and cooking the chicken, steak, bacon, and eggs as early as the day before. Store in separate containers in the refrigerator until 15 minutes before salad is ready to assemble.

SIDE:
SWEET POTATO FRIES WITH DIP

Serves 8

Ingredients You'll Need

For Fries

    12 large sweet potatoes
    3 tablespoons olive oil
    3 teaspoons chili powder
    1 teaspoon sea salt
    1/2 teaspoon garlic powder

For Dip

    1 cup sour cream
    1/2 tablespoon lemon juice (half a lemon)
    2 teaspoons yellow mustard, prepared
    1 teaspoon garlic powder
    1 teaspoon sea salt
    1/2 teaspoon black pepper, freshly ground
    1 cup avocado oil or extra virgin olive oil

Tools You'll Need

    Baking sheet
    Foil
    Cutting board
    Knife
    Measuring spoons
    Silicone spatula
    Food processor or blender
    Citrus juicer (optional)

How to Make It

1. Preheat oven to 450 degrees Fahrenheit.
2. Cover a baking sheet with foil. Set aside.
3. Scrub sweet potatoes thoroughly and dry. Cut unpeeled sweet potatoes into thin slices—aim for slightly less than 1/4 inch thick. The thinner the better!

4. Combine seasonings in a bowl.
5. Place sliced sweet potatoes on the baking sheet in a single layer, and drizzle with olive oil and toss to coat. Then sprinkle with spice mixture. Toss again to coat.
6. Place in preheated oven for 25 minutes, flipping them over halfway through.
7. When 20 minutes are up, turn broiler to high and let potatoes crisp for 1–2 minutes, but watch carefully so they don't burn!
8. For dipping sauce, add all dip ingredients except oil into a food processor or blender. Blend 30 seconds or until ingredients are combined.
9. Add avocado oil (or olive oil) in a thin stream until fully combined.
10. Test for seasoning, and add more lemon juice or salt and pepper if desired.
11. Serve fries fresh out of the oven with dipping sauce.

Recipe Notes

- Make ahead: The dipping sauce will keep in the fridge for a week.
- This dipping sauce also can be used as a homemade, eggless mayo substitute.

DESSERT:
BEST-EVER CHOCOLATE CHUNK COOKIES

Serves 8–10

Ingredients You'll Need

1 1/2 cups all-purpose flour
1/2 teaspoon baking soda
1/4 teaspoon sea salt
8 tablespoons butter, extra soft
1/2 cup granulated sugar
1/4 cup brown sugar
1 teaspoon vanilla
1 egg
3/4 cup semi-sweet chocolate chunks or chips

Tools You'll Need

Baking sheet
Parchment paper
Measuring cups
Measuring spoons
Large mixing bowl
Wooden spoon
Sifter (optional)
Small microwave-safe bowl
Handheld or stand mixer

How to Make It

1. Preheat the oven to 350 degrees Fahrenheit.
2. Line baking sheet with parchment paper. Set aside.
3. In a large mixing bowl, mix (and sift, if possible) flour, baking soda, and salt. Set aside.
4. Depending on how soft your butter is, microwave in a small micro-wave-safe bowl for between 15 and 30 seconds. The butter should be almost completely melted, but do not let it reach hot liquid form. If that happens, save the hot butter for another use (you can let it solidify again in the fridge) and start over.
5. Using a handheld or stand mixer, beat the butter and both sugars on medium until just combined.
6. Incorporate the vanilla and egg on a low speed until just combined.
7. Add flour mixture to wet mixture and beat on low until just combined.
8. Stir in the chocolate chunks (or chips) with a wooden spoon.
9. Form dough into 8–10 balls, and place on your prepared baking sheet.
10. Bake for 10–12 minutes. The cookies will be pale and puffy even when they are done.
11. Cool for 10 minutes (if people can wait that long!).

Recipe Notes

•   Although many chocolate-chip cookies look golden and crispy, these will be pale and puffy.
•   To have these cookies turn out perfectly, do not overbeat the ingredients, and do not overbake. Allowing them to cool for a while gives them a chance to set and will deliver the best chocolate chunk cookie ever.

CHAPTER 7

Waiting Well

Anxiety is the greatest evil
that can befall a soul, except sin.
God commands you to pray,
but he forbids you to worry.

—St. Francis de Sales

Is it just me, or does life seem to be a waiting game? Waiting at the stoplight. Waiting for Christmas. Waiting for the job offer to come through. Waiting for the test result. Waiting for the package to arrive. Whatever the wait is, it's usually on a sliding scale of nerve-wracking to aggravating—and requires a ton of patience.

As a child I viewed patience as something that meant being quiet and still, like how you would sit in the waiting room at the doctor's office. Over the years I have come to understand that this is not patience, but passivity. True patience requires active hope. This active hope is endurance through the times of trial. This spirit of hopeful endurance fights off apathy and keeps you in a state of empowerment, because it pushes you to control your thoughts and regulate your emotions. There is always something to be done, whether it's a prayer to be prayed or something of value to focus on, even if it's as simple as going for a walk or making something good in the kitchen. This active hope is imbued with a sense of having done the best you could, acknowledging the difficulty at hand, and then choosing not to be overcome. It's the difference between having a wishbone and having a backbone.

This version of patience is hard to come by because it's not considered a *virtue du jour*. In a time when immediacy is king—manifested in things like fast food and same-day free shipping—waiting can be a bit countercultural. I discovered this when my husband and I decided to wait to find out whether our first child was a boy or a girl. When people learned we were going for the surprise, many were disappointed or even a little annoyed. Why would you wait when you had the option not to? It was a good question, and one I started to wonder myself halfway through my pregnancy! But it taught me a thing or two about waiting well.

During the middle of my pregnancy one of my younger sisters came out for a visit. She was waiting for something too—the results of her LSAT. It was a week before she would find out her score, and of course, the score would determine whether she'd be accepted to law school. My sister's journey up to that point had been one of a college graduate who went into a field that she couldn't see herself in forever, so she set her sights on the law. She didn't choose it arbitrarily: she had spent a year going to daily Mass and praying specifically for what direction to take with her future. I felt confident that she would pass her LSAT with flying colors because she had always been a stand-out student, but alas, we were bound to wait.

To fend off anxiety, we made Nutella banana bread. (When in doubt, always make Nutella banana bread!) Then we sat and chatted as the bread baked to perfection. Before either of us could wonder aloud what the future would hold, we diverted our thoughts by reading my daily devotional, which happened to have the absolute perfect story for our waiting situation.

The story made reference to St. Paul and his faithful friend, St. Silas, in Acts 16, when they were assailed by a violent mob and thrown into prison. Things looked dark, both figuratively, as they likely would be going to their deaths, and literally, because they were jailed in the innermost part of the dungeon, with their feet fastened to a stake so they couldn't even walk around the cell. What did Paul and Silas do? Did they freak out and start crying? Did they demand answers from God? Did they ask each other over and over again if they would ever be free? The Bible tells us what they did. At midnight, "Paul and Silas were praying and singing hymns to God as the prisoners listened" (Acts 16:25). My sister and I marveled at this together. Not only were they singing praises to God; they were comforting others while they themselves suffered and waited. Then God decided to shake things up. "There was suddenly such a severe earthquake that the foundations of the jail shook; all the doors flew open, and the chains of all were pulled loose" (Acts 16:26). They were free and were able to continue preaching the Gospel.

This encouraging passage gave us pause. Paul and Silas had active hope. They were focused on God, not petitioning him (which is what I often default to!) but *praising* him. Their example is an exhortation to be prayer warriors, not worriers. My little sis and I got to talking about how so much of the frustration of waiting has to do with fearing the end result will not go according to our plan. Of course this is a natural inclination, but it's one that needs to be reexamined through a spiritual lens. We tend to focus so much on what we expect for our story, but what about God's story? Interestingly enough, the word *wait* means not only "to expect" but also "to serve"—to wait on someone, like being waited on at a restaurant. This element of selflessness and service must be present in active hope. We are waiting on God to come through for us, yes, but we should also be waiting on God, asking him how we can best serve.

Days later, when I dropped my sister off at the airport, we parted ways with hugs and hopeful hearts. The wait was almost over, as she was scheduled to find out her score the very next day. As I drove home, I was thinking of how uncertainty, when tethered to active hope, keeps us closer to God. For me, finding out the sex of our child early would lead to more newborn outfits with certain colors, and it would allow for a little more clarity on a name, but strangely the waiting added a new dimension of dependence on God. He knew what I didn't, and I was okay with that.

The next day my sister found out some good news. She rocked the LSAT, which paved the path for her to go to law school, and she has since gone on to practice law. We often think back on that summer as one for the books. We both were at the advent of brand-new and exciting life chapters, and yet we were so unsure of how it would all go. A few months later, eleven days before the due date, our baby was born. At the birth, my husband was the one to declare the big news: "It's a girl!" I remember absorbing the surprise—our baby girl—with awe. I was glad to have waited.

Flannery O'Connor put it best when she wrote, "Don't let me ever think, dear God, that I was anything but the instrument for Your story." To be an instrument in *God's story*: that framing helps provide the mooring to wait well, and it has become a touchstone for me in times of struggle or serenity—along with some Nutella banana bread.

Prayer for Gathering

Actiones Nostras is a traditional Catholic prayer found in the Divine Office (Liturgy of the Hours).

> Lord, may everything we do begin with your inspiration and continue with your help so that all our prayers and works may begin in you and by you be happily ended. We ask this through Christ our Lord. Amen.

Conclude by saying the Our Father.

Prompts for Conversation

- When have you been tested with waiting?
- Are you tempted with a desire for immediacy? At what times?
- What are your thoughts on the following quote from Flannery O'Connor? "Don't let me ever think, dear God, that I was anything but the instrument for Your story."

Menu:
Summer "No-Grill" Barbecue

Although I absolutely love barbecue (Kansas City roots, y'all), I am no grill master. This is why I love a summer menu that enlists the oven to do most of the work. See what I mean when you have these oven ribs practically making themselves! Entertain your guests with a refreshing dill dip in personal pumpernickel bowls. Dijon fingerling potato salad (a nice break from the usual variety) serves as the side. As a finale, serve Nutella banana bread, which is unanimously loved by kids and adults alike.

Starter: Dill Dip with Mini Pumpernickel Bowls
Main: Oven Barbecue Ribs
Side: Mustard Fingerling Potato Salad
Dessert: Nutella Banana Bread

STARTER:
DILL DIP WITH
MINI PUMPERNICKEL BOWLS

Serves 8

There's something so summery about dill dip with veggies and a pumpernickel bowl, but the downside is that no one can enjoy the pumpernickel bowl since doing so would destroy the dip reservoir! That's where these pumpernickel rolls come in and save the day. You can offer your guests their own personal dip bowl by hollowing out the center of each roll and filling it with the creamy dill dip. Stick a few veggies in for decorative garnish, and you have a much-needed update on a fan favorite.

Ingredients You'll Need

8 pumpernickel rolls
1 cup sour cream

1 cup mayonnaise
2 tablespoons dried dill
2 tablespoons dried onion
1 tablespoon dried parsley
1 teaspoon garlic powder
1 teaspoon black pepper, freshly ground
1/8 teaspoon sea salt

For Dipping

Carrot sticks
Snow peas
Mini bell peppers

Tools You'll Need

Measuring cups
Measuring spoons
Medium mixing bowl
Wooden spoon
Plastic wrap

How to Make It

1. Combine all dip ingredients in a medium bowl using a wooden spoon. Cover and chill for at least 30 minutes before serving, but preferably twenty-four hours to allow flavors to meld.
2. When ready to serve, cut a hole in the top of each roll and hollow out to create a reservoir for the dip.
3. Fill the rolls with dip and serve with vegetables of choice, adding a few to each bowl for garnish.

Recipe Notes

- Make ahead: You can store this dip in an airtight container in the refrigerator for up to 3 days.

MAIN:
OVEN BARBECUE RIBS

Serves 8

Ingredients You'll Need

4 (2 to 2 1/2-pound) racks of spare ribs (estimate about a pound of
  ribs per person)
2 cups brown sugar
4 tablespoons chili powder
4 teaspoons garlic powder
4 teaspoons sea salt
1 teaspoon ground cinnamon
Several cranks freshly ground black pepper
Barbecue sauce, such as Lillie's Q, Bone Suck'n Sauce, or Trader Joe's
  (optional)

Tools You'll Need

Baking sheet
Aluminum foil
Small mixing bowl
Fork
Measuring cups
Measuring spoons

How to Make It

1. Heat oven to one of the following temperatures based on the amount
   of time you have to make the ribs: 2 1/2 to 3 hours at 300 degrees Fahrenheit, or 3 1/2 to 4 hours at 250 degrees.
2. Line a baking sheet with foil.
3. In a small mixing bowl, combine brown sugar, chili powder, garlic
   powder, salt, and cinnamon.
4. Place each slab of ribs on a large piece of foil. Generously pat the spice
   rub onto each side of the ribs and then place meat side down on the
   foil. Tightly fold the foil over to make sealed packets.

5. Bake in oven according to the times and temperatures outlined in the first step. The ribs will be falling off the bone when done. Cut the slabs in fourths or cut ribs individually and serve with barbecue sauce on the side; or serve without sauce, as these are perfect by themselves.

SIDE:
MUSTARD FINGERLING POTATO SALAD

Serves 8

Ingredients You'll Need

4 pounds fingerling potatoes
2 (9-ounce) bags sugar snap peas
8 radishes, thinly sliced
1/4 cup green onions, finely chopped

For Mustard Vinaigrette

1/2 cup olive oil
4 tablespoons whole-grain mustard
4 teaspoons Dijon mustard
4 tablespoons rice vinegar or white wine vinegar
1 tablespoon honey
Sea salt, to taste
Black pepper, freshly ground, to taste

Tools You'll Need

Large saucepan
Fork
Slotted spoon
Cutting board
Knife
Measuring cups
Measuring spoons
Serving bowl
Small mixing bowl

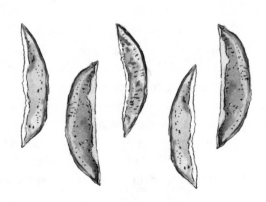

Whisk
Plastic wrap

How to Make It

1. To prepare the potatoes, scrub them clean and then place in a large saucepan with cold water to just cover them.
2. Turn heat to high and bring water to a boil, cooking potatoes for 15 minutes. Test at this point with a fork. The fork should pierce through the potatoes with ease; if not, keep boiling a few more minutes.
3. Remove potatoes from water with a slotted spoon and place them on a plate to cool.
4. Empty the potato water from the saucepan and refill with 2 inches of water. Bring to a boil and add a dash of salt along with the sugar snap peas. The peas should turn bright green and be cooked after 2 minutes.
5. Remove the peas with a slotted spoon and place on a cutting board. Pat dry with a towel, and cut the snap peas into three segments.
6. Chop the vegetables: finely slice the radishes and green onions, and cut the potatoes into fourths. Add all to the serving bowl.
7. Whisk the dressing ingredients together in a small mixing bowl and add more salt and pepper if necessary (it will likely be necessary). If the dressing is too sharp for your taste, add more honey in increments of 1 tablespoon at a time.
8. Prior to serving—at least 30 minutes before—toss the veggies and dressing. Cover and keep at room temperature before serving.

Recipe Notes

- Make ahead: The mustard vinaigrette can be made the day before and all the vegetables can be prepared then as well. Store in separate containers in the refrigerator, and then follow the last step: toss the salad with dressing and bring to room temperature 30 minutes before serving.

DESSERT:
NUTELLA BANANA BREAD

Serves 8

This is my husband's favorite. It can be thrown together in no time at all and is the perfect treat for so many different occasions—everything from a social, to a bake sale, to a housewarming gift. When in doubt, make Nutella banana bread.

Ingredients You'll Need

> 6 tablespoons butter, melted
> 3 extremely ripe bananas, mashed
> 2 eggs
> 3/4 cup sour cream or plain yogurt
> 2 teaspoons vanilla extract
> 2 cups all-purpose flour
> 1 teaspoon baking soda
> 1 teaspoon sea salt
> 3/4 cup granulated sugar
> 2/3 cup Nutella

Tools You'll Need

> Bread loaf pan (9x5 inch)
> Parchment paper
> Saucepan or microwave-safe dish
> 2 large mixing bowls
> Wooden spoon
> Knife
> Toothpick

How to Make It

1. Preheat oven to 350 degrees Fahrenheit.
2. Line a bread loaf pan with parchment paper.
3. Melt the butter in the microwave or in saucepan on the stove.

4. In a large mixing bowl, mash the bananas with a wooden spoon. Add the melted butter, along with the eggs, sour cream, and vanilla. Stir until just combined. Set aside.
5. In a different bowl, combine the dry ingredients: flour, baking soda, salt, and sugar.
6. Add dry ingredients to banana mixture and stir with a wooden spoon until just combined.
7. Microwave Nutella for 20 seconds. It should be a softened consistency but not melted.
8. Pour half of the batter into the prepared loaf pan, and add half of Nutella amount to the top of the batter, using a knife to make swirls in the banana mixture.
9. Add the last half of the batter and repeat swirls with remaining Nutella.
10. Bake for 50 minutes, or until it passes the toothpick test.
11. Cool 15 minutes and remove from the pan.

CHAPTER 8

Time to Gather

Nothing you have not given
away will ever really be yours.

–C. S. Lewis, *Mere Christianity*

In Ireland, when a gathering is hosted, an old custom dictates that guests should never arrive empty-handed or, as the Irish saying goes, "with your arms at the one length" (hanging empty at your sides). I would agree, and furthermore I'd argue that this is good practice anywhere in the world. This Irish gold standard can apply to our spiritual life. We do not want to show up at heaven's gate with our arms at one length. What we give away to others is what we will be allowed to bring across that magnificent threshold—the bounty of what we were willing to give away during life.

Giving comes in many different forms. One can give but be stingy. One can give generously but do so begrudgingly. One can give from what little they have, and it is a bigger gift than what someone gives from a surplus. The act of giving plays a big role in scripture; in fact the first story we have in Genesis post-Eden is about God's judgment of two gifts—those offered by brothers, Cain and Abel. "In the course of time Cain brought an offering to the LORD from the fruit of the ground, while Abel, for his part, brought the fatty portion of the firstlings of his flock. The LORD looked with favor on Abel and his offering, but on Cain and his offering he did not look with favor. So Cain was very angry and dejected" (Gn 4:3–5). Theologians have speculated as to why Cain's offering was rejected. A common thought is that because Abel's offering was the "fatty portion of the firstlings of his flock," it was the best portion of the animal and showed that Abel brought his utmost to the Lord.[1] Another view is that Cain's offering was rejected because he did not present a blood sacrifice, which was the greatest form of sacrifice. Today, God isn't asking us for a gift of blood sacrifice (thankfully!), but he does want the first fruits of our heart, and when we give, it should stretch us a little.

For me, one of the most challenging ways to give is my time. I think we would all agree that there may be nothing more personal or taxing than devoting one's time to something. Time is so valuable that people are paid by the hour, and nothing is quite so irritating as when something is a "waste of time." I used to think of giving my time along the lines of volunteering, being involved with the parish, working on a project, or going out to support someone, but I came to realize that making time for gathering deserved a place on the list.

Gathering emphasizes "we time" as opposed to "me time." These days, "we time" is at an all-time low, and loneliness is reaching an all-time high. Loneliness is now considered an epidemic in America, after an extensive study conducted in 2018 found that over 50 percent of people consistently felt "alone or left out."[2] Even more respondents said "no one knows them well." And still more felt as if those around them "are not necessarily with them." The study also revealed that many people lacked companionship in life, that interpersonal relationships lacked meaning, and that people generally felt isolated from others. The most surprising aspect of the study was that for the first time, young people (millennials and Generation Z) were lonelier than their older counterparts.

I remember feeling lonely during the transition from graduating college to entering the "real world" with my first job. I felt like the new kid on the first day of school, which is never a fun feeling. I was grateful when a coworker invited me to a gathering she hosted weekly—a prayer group—and so I accepted the invitation and attended the following week. The Irish in me made sure my arms were not "at the one length," and I arrived with a pan of homemade brownies (a surefire way to make new friends!). Most of the young people there were also in the entertainment industry and proved extremely welcoming. We prayed the Rosary and afterward simply talked. One guy told me that it had taken him years after working in Los Angeles to really find a community, and specifically to meet the people who were all present that evening. I felt happy to have come across such a nice bunch, and little did I know their fellowship would be a big part of my life for years to come.

A decade later, I was the new kid on the block once again. My husband and I had moved to the East Coast, and we were in the process of putting down roots and getting to know people. The parish we attended had a couples group, and a volunteer opportunity arose to host a monthly gathering. I felt a little nervous because I didn't know anyone, but I thought back to the invitation I had received so many years before that had yielded so many great memories. I decided to go for it and put our name down for the following month. We hosted a wine-cheese-charcuterie night, and after I finished obsessing over making sure there would be enough food and that the wine pairings were just right, all that was left was for people to show up! If you're the hostess (or host), there's that moment when you're practically holding your breath before the first person arrives, especially when you don't know the people who are coming. The suspense was soon over when guests did indeed make an appearance. At the end of the night my husband and I were glad we hosted. We met some cool people and had some great conversations, all because we were willing to stretch a little.

When it comes to gathering, there's always a million excuses *not* to put in the effort: *Do we really have the time? What if everyone's out of town that weekend? Shouldn't we wait until the couch gets recovered?* The gathering doesn't have to be a Gatsby-grade party in order to be wonderful. In the end gathering is about rising to the occasion in order to make the occasion. It is a small act of generosity to host or to attend. It's an act of faith not to hold your time too tightly, and it's an act of generosity to reach out—and when you do reach out to others it's impossible to keep your "arms at the one length." You'll find that what you gave away in time, you'll gain back in grace and friendship a hundredfold. It's always worth making time to gather together.

Prayer for Gathering

Prayer for Generosity attributed to St. Ignatius of Loyola

Lord, teach me to be generous,
to serve you as you deserve,
to give and not to count the cost,
to fight and not to heed the wounds,
to toil and not to seek for rest,
to labor and not to look for any reward,
save that of knowing that I do your holy will.

Conclude by saying the Our Father.

Prompts for Conversation

- Are you tempted to hold on to your time too tightly? How?
- Have you seen evidence of or can you attest personally to the statistics mentioned about loneliness?
- What is the ideal way you enjoy hanging out with people? Could you make more time for that?

Menu:
Wine and Cheese Social

Perhaps there's nothing simpler, or classier, than a charcuterie and cheese board. Charcuterie is the French culinary tradition of making pork products such as sausages, salami, and prosciutto. A charcuterie and cheese board always has four basic elements: cheese, meats, fruit, and bread. Below are suggestions to build your own fabulous board, along with drinks and dessert.

Starter: Wine and Elderflower Mocktail
Main and Side: Charcuterie and Cheese Board
Dessert: Flourless Chocolate Cake

STARTER: WINE AND ELDERFLOWER MOCKTAIL

WINE

How Much

When determining how much wine to have on hand, a good rule of thumb is to plan on two drinks per person in the first hour and one drink every hour after that.

Pairing

Pairing wine with a variety of cheeses can be difficult because there are so many specific recommendations for different kinds of cheese. A good tip is to avoid "oaky" wines. If you want to choose a red and a white, try a Pinot

Noir and semi-dry Riesling. Champagne, cava, or sparkling rosé can also be lovely complements to most cheeses. Serve what you like best!

Nonalcoholic Beverage

Sparkling water is a must for all your guests. Have several bottles chilled and glasses at the ready. Additionally, it is important to have a special non-alcoholic beverage for those who will not be drinking wine. The following Elderflower Mocktail is perfect because it will not overpower the cheese and has some bubbles.

ELDERFLOWER MOCKTAIL

Serves 8

Ingredients You'll Need

Elderflower cordial (16.9 ounces), available at most liquor stores
4 lemons, cut into fourths with any seeds removed
8 (10-ounce) club sodas, chilled
Ice

Tools You'll Need

Citrus juicer
Utensil for stirring

How to Make It

1. For each mocktail: fill glass with ice, and add 2 tablespoons of elder-flower cordial.
2. Squeeze the juice of a lemon quarter into each glass.
3. Top off glass with club soda and stir.

Recipe Notes

- Test this beforehand to make sure the taste is right, and add more elderflower cordial or lemon juice to taste.
- You could also make this in a pitcher. Pour in a fourth of the cordial and the juice of 3 lemons, and fill the rest with club soda. Stir and taste for adjustments.

MAIN AND SIDE:
CHARCUTERIE AND CHEESE BOARD

Tools You'll Need

Serving platters such as a large ceramic platter, marble slab, slate board, wooden cutting board, or a big sheet of butcher block paper (that way you can write the names of the cheese on it so people know what they're having!)

Cheese knives

Charcuterie

The rule of thumb is to serve 2 ounces of meat per person, and 5 ounces if it's the sole food source at a gathering that serves as dinner. Try serving three meats with different textures:

Salami (hard)

Prosciutto (soft)

Chorizo (cured sausage)

Cheese

Consider a combination of soft and hard cheeses, and always include two cheeses that most people universally like, such as cheddar, mozzarella, Gouda, or Parmesan. For the firm cheeses, slice in advance. It is also a good idea to give each cheese its own cheese knife so the flavors don't mingle. And last but not least, always serve cheese at room temperature, so remember to remove from fridge a half hour before your guests arrive. Select three to five cheeses for your board based on the different categories and your taste!

Soft: Brie, mozzarella, burrata

Semi-soft: Gouda, Gorgonzola, Stilton

Semi-firm: aged sharp cheddar, Gouda, provolone

Firm: Gruyère, Manchego, Parmigiano-Reggiano

Crumbly: chèvre

More Ideas to Build Your Ultimate Board

Pick and choose from some of the following options:

OLIVES

For the olives, ideally select ones that are pitted. If not, warn your guests!

Castellano, bright green and sweet
Cerignola, crisp and buttery
Manzanilla, smoky and nutty

SPREADS

Pepper jelly (amazing)
Balsamic fig spread
Mustards, Dijon or grainy
Honey with honeycomb
Hummus

FRUITS AND NUTS

Champagne grapes, cut into small bunches
Dried apricots
Dried mandarins
Figs
Apples, fresh sliced or dried
Cherries
Pistachios
Salted almonds
Rosemary marcona almonds
Spicy pecans
Sugared nuts of any kind

VEGETABLES

Grilled artichoke hearts, from a jar (drained)
Hot and sweet cherry peppers, from a jar (drained)
Cornichons
Mini bell peppers
Baby carrots

BREAD

Crusty French bread
Pumpernickel pretzels
Breadsticks
Cheese straws

Everything crackers

Seasonal crisps, such as rosemary, fig, or pumpkin from Trader Joe's

SWEETS

Chocolate peanut-butter cups

Chocolate pistachio bark

Chocolate-covered pretzels

Almonds covered in dark chocolate and sea salt

Stroopwafels

Bars of dark chocolate with an interesting flavor combination, broken
up

DESSERT:
FLOURLESS CHOCOLATE CAKE

Serves 8

Merging low-maintenance and elegance, this cake has a rich chocolate taste
and is a tad more sophisticated than your typical frosted chocolate cake. It's
the perfect high note on which to end a wine and cheese social.

Ingredients You'll Need

2 teaspoons flour of choice, for flouring the cake pan

1 cup semi-sweet chocolate chips

1/2 cup butter, *unsalted*, plus 1 tablespoon butter for greasing pan

3/4 cup granulated sugar

3 large eggs, slightly beaten

1/4 teaspoon sea salt

1 teaspoon vanilla extract

1/2 cup unsweetened cocoa powder

Powdered sugar, for dusting

Optional Garnishes

Whipped cream

Strawberries or raspberries

Tools You'll Need

Round cake pan (8 inch)
Parchment paper
Pencil
Scissors
Measuring cups
Measuring spoons
Saucepan
Wooden spoon
Toothpick
Wire cooling rack
Sifter
Cake plate

How to Make It

1. Preheat oven to 375 degrees Fahrenheit.
2. Grease an 8-inch round cake pan with butter and then dust with flour. Take parchment paper, and with a pencil trace a circle using the bottom of the cake pan. Cut the circle out with scissors and fit it in the base of the cake pan. Grease and flour the top of the parchment. Set pan aside.
3. Place chocolate chips and butter in a saucepan on medium heat, stirring often with a wooden spoon until melted and smooth.
4. Into the saucepan, add the sugar, eggs, salt, and vanilla, stirring until smooth. Add the cocoa powder until just combined. Pour batter into the prepared cake pan.
5. Bake for 25 minutes, or until a toothpick is inserted and comes out clean.
6. Allow the cake to cool for 10 minutes on a wire rack.
7. With a sifter, dust powdered sugar on top of the cake for decorative effect.
8. Serve with garnish if you wish: whipped cream, strawberries, or raspberries (or all three!).

Recipe Notes

• The cake is gluten-free. If you want to avoid gluten for dietary reasons, be sure to use gluten-free flour to dust the cake pan.

CHAPTER 9

Eternal Wealth

> How can there be too many
> children? That is like saying there
> are too many flowers.
>
> —St. Teresa of Calcutta

I was at my baby shower, sipping a steaming cup of chamomile tea, while I stood next to my three sisters—and one very vocal guest—who informed us that "only the biggest idiots have big families." Ah. Did she know we came from a family of seven? Maybe it slipped her mind. We nodded politely and filed it in the mental dustbin (along with all the other crumpled comments we have received our whole lives for coming from a "big family").

My parents are a couple who looked upon each child as a gift; they both had the goal of creating a family that would be loving and godly and one that would stand as a strong support system. As the oldest child (with my youngest brother fourteen years my junior), I remember my mother telling me that my siblings would be the "greatest blessings one day," and to be quite honest, I found it a *little* hard to believe that the kid who was giving me attitude when I babysat would be my future best friend. But was she ever right.

The best way I can describe coming from a big family is that it is pro-life as opposed to pro-lifestyle—it's a world of relationship and focusing on the other. This is a countercultural concept in a self-absorbed world that is obsessed with the tally marks of how many likes you get on the latest social media, or spending money on something new to flaunt in front of your friends. My family approached life, not by what we might not have, but with a spirit of "Enough is as good as a feast."

A myth surrounding big families is that somehow people won't be properly cared for or that there's not enough attention to go around. While I can't speak to every family situation, I can confidently say that my brothers and sisters and I were always cared for physically, emotionally, spiritually, and materially. In fact, we probably got more attention than usual because there were three times the normal amount of people in the house to give love. For this very reason, I always appreciated the movie *Yours, Mine and Ours* (the version with Lucille Ball and Henry Fonda), where the father says at the climax of the film:

> It's giving life that counts. Until you're ready for it, all the rest is just a big fraud. All the crazy haircuts in the world won't keep it turning. Life isn't a love-in, it's the dishes and the orthodontist and the shoe repairman and . . . ground round instead of roast beef. And I'll tell you something else: it isn't going to bed with a man that proves you're in love with him; it's getting up in the morning and facing the drab, miserable, wonderful everyday world with him that counts. . . . I suppose having nineteen kids is carrying it a bit too far, but if we had it to do over, who would we skip . . . you?"[1]

I can't think of one material thing on any level that I would trade for a brother or sister. But that's not the message the world pumps into the pipeline. Whether it's on TV, over the radio, or on the cover of a magazine, we're constantly reminded of what we don't have. That messaging fuels a steady burning fear of missing out—that somehow if we don't have everything we want, it will be a dark world of misery and discontent.

I would argue the opposite. I think when you do get everything you want, it is a world of misery and discontent. Nothing is waited for, and so nothing is special. When you have to wait for things—whether it's to take a turn on the swing in the backyard, or to get a car when you're ready to drive—it creates a spirit of sufficiency instead of scarcity. It teaches you to set yourself aside for another, maybe a little begrudgingly at first, but then out of love, with the knowledge that the world doesn't revolve around you—because guess what? It doesn't. Family done well impresses upon a soul that not only do you have enough; you are enough. You are valued for you.

Not only do you learn the value of the individual in a big family, but you learn the power of the group. I remember the summer my siblings and I were tasked with repainting our white picket fence. It was like something out of *The Adventures of Tom Sawyer*: kids armed with paintbrushes and assigned different sections to maximize efforts in hopes to finish in record time. Of course, there was a reward waiting—a big screen TV. Yes, my dad knew how to put the proverbial carrot before the horse, and so we all worked like madmen, me leading the charge and scowling at any sibling who took excessive water breaks. What my dad thought would take at least a week took us two and a half days. The adage of "many hands make light work" delivered, and then Dad had to deliver on the TV. This memory encapsulates the beauty of family bonding together to do something great, and that is what family is all about.

My parents would be the first to tell you that it wasn't always easy. They had to work hard, and they achieved more than any couple I know of while raising a big family: managing a law practice, professorship, and an international ministry, as well as helping every child, one of whom had dyslexia, all the way through college. It's surreal to think back on the days when people would come over to our house, in the years when everyone was home, and say that our family was like something out of a sitcom: kids running every which way, singing, talking, playing, laughing. Yes, my parents' hands were full, and they still are—they are full of blessings. As the Irish proverb that hangs in my mother's kitchen reads: "For wealth is family and family is wealth." I hope to follow their example.

Prayer for Gathering

A Prayer for the Family by St. Teresa of Calcutta[2]

Heavenly Father, you have given us the model of life in the Holy Family of Nazareth. Help us, O Loving Father, to make our family another Nazareth where love, peace and joy reign. May it be deeply contemplative, intensely eucharistic, revived with joy. Help us to stay together in joy and sorrow in family prayer. Teach us to see Jesus in the members of our families, especially in their distressing disguise. May the eucharistic heart of Jesus make our hearts humble like his and help us to carry out our family duties in a holy way. May we love one another as God loves each one of us, more and more each day, and forgive each other's faults as you forgive our sins. Help us, O Loving Father, to take whatever you give and give whatever you take with a big smile.

Immaculate Heart of Mary, cause of our joy, pray for us.

St. Joseph, pray for us.

Holy Guardian Angels, be always with us, guide and protect us. Amen.

Conclude by saying the Our Father.

Prompts for Conversation

- What are your thoughts on the following proverb? "For wealth is family and family is wealth."
- What does family mean to you?
- For you, what does it mean to be pro-life versus pro-lifestyle?

Menu:
Back-to-School Dinner

This menu will forever remind me of going back to school because my mom would make it often during that time of year. The honey-curried chicken with garlic rice is as delicious as it is simple. The mandarin-chèvre-blueberry salad is my favorite salad, and the brown-butter rice crispies are a salty twist on a childhood bake-sale classic.

Starter: Mandarin-Chèvre-Blueberry Salad
Main: Honey-Curried Chicken
Side: Garlic Rice
Dessert: Brown-Butter Crispies with Sea Salt

STARTER:
MANDARIN-CHÈVRE-BLUEBERRY SALAD

Adapted from Joanna Gaines: "Jo's Quick Table Salad"[3]
Serves 8
This salad has a delightful array of flavors that accents the honey-curried chicken and garlic rice. The sweetness of the mandarins, the richness of the goat cheese, and the tartness of the blueberries are delicious. I could live on this.

Ingredients You'll Need

2 (9-ounce) bags romaine lettuce
2 (11-ounce) cans of mandarin oranges, drained
1 cup dried blueberries
1/2 cup spicy-sweet pecans
   (or any sugared nut)
1 cup chèvre (goat cheese), crumbled

For Dressing
>   1/2 cup olive oil
>   4 tablespoons red wine vinegar
>   2 tablespoons honey
>   1/2 teaspoon sea salt
>   1/2 teaspoon black pepper, freshly ground
>   Dash of hot sauce

Tools You'll Need

>   Serving bowl
>   Whisk
>   Can opener

How to Make It

1. Whisk dressing ingredients together in the bowl you plan to use to serve the salad. (I'm all for saving on doing dishes!)
2. Before serving, add lettuce and mandarins to the bowl of dressing and toss to coat evenly.
3. Sprinkle the blueberries, nuts, and crumbled goat cheese on top.

MAIN:
HONEY-CURRIED CHICKEN

Adapted from Suzanne Fowler: "Golden Glazed Chicken"[4]
Serves 8

Ingredients You'll Need

>   Sea salt and freshly ground black pepper, for seasoning
>   8 chicken breasts (ideally the thin-sliced ones, so each person can have their own)
>   1/2 cup butter, plus 2 tablespoons for greasing pans
>   1 cup honey
>   1/2 cup Dijon mustard, grainy
>   4 tablespoons yellow mustard
>   4 teaspoons curry powder

1 teaspoon sea salt
2 cloves of garlic, minced or pressed

Tools You'll Need

2 baking dishes (9x13 inch)
Measuring cups
Measuring spoons
Saucepan
Heatproof spoon
Meat thermometer

How to Make It

1. Preheat oven to 350 degrees Fahrenheit.
2. Butter the 9x13 inch dishes. Salt and pepper the chicken breasts. Place in the baking dishes.
3. In a small saucepan combine the rest of the ingredients, stirring with a heatproof spoon until melted and smooth.
4. Pour the curry sauce over the chicken.
5. Bake in the oven for 30–35 minutes or until the internal temperature reads 165 degrees with a meat thermometer.

Recipe Notes

- When preparing the plates, place the chicken on a generous bed of garlic rice. Ladle the remaining cooked sauce from the baking dish over the chicken and rice. Serve salad on the side.

SIDE:
GARLIC RICE

Serves 8

Ingredients You'll Need

8 tablespoons salted butter, divided
4 cloves garlic, minced or pressed
3 cups white rice
5 cups chicken stock
1/2 cup green onions, finely chopped
Sea salt and freshly ground black pepper, to taste

Tools You'll Need

Saucepan with lid
Garlic press
Measuring spoons
Measuring cups
Heatproof spoon
Serving bowl

How to Make It

1. In a large saucepan, heat 4 tablespoons of butter on medium-high heat until melted. Add garlic and cook for 1 minute until it begins to brown. Add rice, and coat in the garlic butter using a heatproof spoon.
2. Add chicken stock and bring to a boil. Turn down to a simmer and cover with lid to cook 12–15 minutes or according to your rice package instructions.
3. The rice is done when the liquid is fully absorbed. Remove from stove. Allow the rice to rest for 10 minutes while keeping the lid on.
4. Transfer rice to serving bowl, and add the rest of the butter and the green onions. Season with sea salt and pepper.

DESSERT: BROWN-BUTTER CRISPIES WITH SEA SALT

Adapted from Deb Perelman: "Salted Brown Butter Crispy Treats"[5]
Serves 8 (plus one extra for taste-testing!)
This recipe elevates the old-fashioned rice crispy treat to one with "grown-up" flare. The sea-salt component and the extra effort of browning the butter take these to the next level. I made these for an office gathering once, and people were sending me emails all day saying they'd never tasted better rice crispie treats!

Ingredients You'll Need

1/2 cup butter, unsalted, plus 1/2 tablespoon to butter the pan
Marshmallows (16-ounce bag)
5–6 cups Rice Krispies or equivalent rice cereal
1/4 teaspoon sea salt (not table salt)
Flaky sea salt for garnish, such as Maldon

Tools You'll Need

8x8 inch square baking dish or pan
Parchment paper
Large pot
Heatproof spoon
Silicone spatula (optional)
Knife
Airtight container

How to Make It

1. Butter the 8x8 inch pan. Press parchment into the corners. Set aside.
2. Begin to melt butter on medium-low heat in a large pot.
3. To brown the butter, allow it to foam, and then wait for it to get clear, stirring occasionally with a heatproof spoon.
4. Watch for small brown bits to form in the clear butter. A word to the wise: be patient, and do not walk away from the pan! The butter should

start to smell nutty and take on a deep golden-brown color. You want to see brown bits, so don't be afraid that it's burning. This can take up to 8 minutes.

5. When you have achieved the browned-butter look, immediately remove the pan from the burner so the brown bits do not go black. (If they burn, you will need to start over.)
6. Stir in the marshmallows until smooth. If you must return the pan to the heat in order to melt the marshmallows, do so on the lowest setting; otherwise, the treats will be stiff.
7. Add the cereal and the salt. Do not be afraid of this salt addition, because it makes all the difference in these treats!
8. Transfer the mixture to the prepared pan, and gently smooth into the corners and even out the top.
9. Allow treats to rest for 30 minutes, and then lift the parchment up and remove the treats from the pan to cut into squares. Sprinkle with flaky sea salt for garnish.

Recipe Notes

- Store in an airtight container if not serving right away.
- If you only have table salt, use slightly less than 1/8 teaspoon.
- If you only have salted butter, only use 1/8 teaspoon of sea salt.
- For the marshmallows, avoid using marshmallows that have tapioca starch. I learned this the hard way. They congeal instead of melting like the traditional marshmallows and therefore will not work for the recipe.

CHAPTER 10

Travelers

The world is a book, and those
who do not travel read only a page.

—St. Augustine

At twenty-five I announced to my family over Christmas that I would be going to Europe the following year. I had always wanted to travel abroad but had never done so, and all of a sudden I wondered what had been stopping me. I didn't have a plan in place, but the first step was to speak life into my goal. God used words to create, and I have found that speaking your hopes has value. The book of Proverbs says, "Death and life are in the power of the tongue; those who choose one shall eat its fruit" (18:21). So in this spirit, I said it would happen and believed it.

Within three days, I got a call from two of my best friends, who had great news. Prior to leaving town for Christmas we had all gone out to dinner with a man who had connections all over the Catholic world due to his work. As we chatted over Italian food in Venice Beach on an unusually cold and rainy California night, it was one of those times when you meet a fellow Catholic and something about them feels like family. Well, for some crazy reason, this man and his wife had decided to give us a generous gift to travel somewhere special—enough to cover flights and all travel expenses. The only stipulation in receiving the gift was that the trip would include some sort of spiritual pilgrimage. Even as I type this now, I can't believe it actually happened.

But it did happen. The year ahead was extremely busy with work, and we all had to agree on where we wanted to visit and find the right time.

Ideas were bandied about: Mexico City, Lourdes, Fatima, but we eventually landed on Rome and Paris. After dodging a bullet of nearly booking flights to Rome in August (we found out *no one* goes to Italy in August), we set our trip for the end of October.

The months flew by, and before we knew it our departure date was fast approaching. This was the time when we should have been planning every detail of our journey, but instead, things were so hectic that all there was time for was booking lodgings. Thankfully we were able to get around to each of our destinations, despite barely having an itinerary and not using cell phones unless we were on Wi-Fi. We explored the cities of Rome, Assisi, Florence, Venice, Paris, Lisieux, and Mont Saint-Michel using old-fashioned handheld maps and public transportation.

This lack of planning allowed for creativity on our journey, since we had not drawn up so many plans beforehand that it would intimidate improvising. Something about this went against the grain, and yet everything about it was blessed. We had some marvelous experiences, including the privilege of filming the International Day of Families in Rome on top of St. Peter's Basilica—a spot that was restricted access and that afforded a view of the Eternal City for miles—where we saw thousands of families gathered below as they released countless colorful balloons into the violet Roman sky. We reveled in the glories of nature while walking the fields of Assisi, the exact places where the holy saints Francis and Clare did too. We were treated to limoncello by strangers as we ate delicious pasta at the most quintessential Italian restaurant of all time, complete with drippy candles and red checkered tablecloths. We sang "O Sacred Head Surrounded" kneeling before the Crown of Thorns in the treasured Cathédrale Notre-Dame. We prayed before the relics of St. Thérèse the Little Flower (my family's special saint), which happened to be on display at Sacré-Cœur, and afterward we reached the Eiffel Tower right as it started to sparkle. I was in awe of how many shining moments came about and that they were all unplanned.

It was our last night in Rome, and we wanted to get to the Colosseum by sunset. We were walking as fast as we could, but knew we wouldn't make it in time, so we ran over to a taxi. I couldn't speak Italian, but could understand enough to know that the taxi driver said he couldn't take us. So we went to another taxi, and we got the same answer. It must not have been worth the trip to them, but it certainly was to us! All we could do was continue on foot. After trekking the ancient cobblestone paths for what seemed like an eternity, we went down a narrow set of stairs that opened up into a courtyard with a basilica. It was a pretty sight as the sun was starting to set, and concertina music floated through the air. Everything was aglow in the waning light, when I discovered that the basilica was one I had heard of before. It was the Basilica of St. Peter in Chains, honoring the time when St. Peter, our first pope, was imprisoned in Jerusalem.

As the story goes, Peter was bound in chains, when his shackles miraculously fell from his wrists and the prison door opened, allowing him to go free. This account is in Acts 12, and it was one that my mom would often reference as an example of how God can do *anything*. She even gave me a gold chain bracelet for my college graduation to serve as a keepsake to remind me of St. Peter's incredible story whenever I clasped it on my wrist. The significance of coming upon this basilica was not lost on me. I saw the actual chains of St. Peter that are displayed in a reliquary, and I touched my bracelet to them for a blessing. It turned out that there was a concert in the basilica taking place that night, too, and so we got to appreciate heavenly music in an earthly house of God.

Later that night, we did eventually make it to the Colosseum (still on foot), but how thankful I was that we had that detour. This trip instilled in me an appreciation for taking life as God sends it to you. If you plan everything out perfectly, it's easy to shut God out, because you *think* you're in control. So much of life is being able to view the unexpected detours as gifts, even when they are outside your plan. It's astonishing how much God will show you if you leave some things up to him.

Prayer for Gathering

Prayer to St. Raphael, patron of travelers, happy meetings, and healing

O Raphael, lead us toward those we are waiting for, those who are waiting for us! Raphael, Angel of Happy Meetings, lead us by the hand toward those we are looking for! May all our movements, all their movements, be guided by your Light and transfigured by your

Joy. Angel Guide of Tobias, lay the request we now address to you at
the feet of him on whose unveiled Face you are privileged to gaze.
Lonely and tired, crushed by the separations and sorrows of earth,
we feel the need of calling to you and of pleading for the protection
of your wings, so that we may not be as strangers in the Province
of Joy, all ignorant of the concerns of our country. Remember the
weak, you who are strong—you whose home lies beyond the region
of thunder, in a land that is always peaceful, always serene, and
bright with the resplendent glory of God. Amen.

Conclude by saying the Our Father.

Prompts for Conversation

- What are your thoughts on the following quote from St. Augustine?
  "The world is a book, and those who do not travel read only a page."
- Share one of your favorite travel experiences.
- Can you think of a time when things turned out better because of a
  detour?

Menu: Fall Feast

This menu fits so well with the crisp weather of autumn—from the roasted butternut squash soup, to a spectacular stuffed pumpkin baked to perfection in the French style. Tell everyone to save room, because a rustic apple crisp is for dessert.

Starter: Roasted Butternut Squash Soup
Main: Spectacular Stuffed Pumpkin
Side: Kale Salad with Cider-Maple Vinaigrette
Dessert: Any-Fruit Crisp with Homemade Caramel Sauce

STARTER:
ROASTED BUTTERNUT SQUASH SOUP

Serves 8

Ingredients You'll Need

4 (12-ounce) packages precut butternut squash (or 2 medium butternut squashes, peeled, seeded, and chopped)
4 tablespoons olive oil, divided
1 tablespoon honey
Sea salt and freshly ground black pepper, for seasoning
1 large onion, chopped
2 cloves garlic, minced or pressed
4 cups chicken or vegetable stock
1 teaspoon sea salt
1/2 teaspoon black pepper, freshly ground
Healthy pinch of ground cinnamon
Healthy pinch of ground nutmeg
2 cups unsweetened canned coconut milk or heavy cream

Optional Garnishes
  Croutons
  Sour Cream
  Paprika
  Hot sauce
  Spiced pumpkin seeds
  Pomegranate seeds
  Brown sugar

Tools You'll Need

  2 baking sheets
  Aluminum foil
  Knife
  Cutting board
  Fork
  Garlic press (optional)
  Measuring cups
  Measuring spoons
  Dutch oven
  Immersion (hand) blender or regular blender (I highly recommend an immersion blender for making soup, as a regular blender can be hazardous when dealing with hot liquids.)

How to Make It

1. Preheat oven to 400 degrees Fahrenheit.
2. Line two baking sheets with foil.
3. Place chopped squash in a single layer on the prepared baking sheets, drizzle with 2 tablespoons of olive oil, honey, and season with salt and pepper. Toss to coat. Roast in oven for 45 minutes.
4. While the squash is roasting, chop the onion and prep the garlic.
5. Heat a tablespoon of olive oil in a Dutch oven over medium-high heat. Add the onion and garlic and sauté for 5–6 minutes. Remove from heat.
6. When squash easily pierces with a fork, it is done. Add it to the Dutch oven along with the stock, salt, pepper, and spices.
7. Place Dutch oven back on the burner and turn to medium-high heat. Bring the soup to a low boil and then reduce heat to medium-low, covering to simmer 20 minutes.

8. When the time is up, stir coconut milk or cream into the mix, and then blend with an immersion blender until smooth. If not using an immersion blender, remove soup from heat for 15 minutes to cool. Once the soup is no longer hot, add to a traditional blender, but do not overfill the blender. Try pureeing half and then removing it to a mixing bowl, and then repeating the process with the remaining mixture. Then add it back into the Dutch oven to reheat on medium heat for 10 minutes.

9. Taste for seasoning and add more salt and pepper if desired.

Recipe Notes

- Make ahead: You can make this soup a day in advance and reheat on the stove at medium heat for 20 minutes prior to serving.
- I highly recommend buying precut squash as it saves time.
- This soup can be dairy-free and vegan if you use vegetable broth and coconut milk.
- Serve with garnishes like sour cream, paprika, hot sauce, spiced pumpkin seeds, or pomegranate seeds.
- If you're serving this soup on its own, a nice addition is homemade croutons. They're a snap to make. Just heat 4 tablespoons of melted butter in a skillet on medium-high heat. Add a few handfuls of cubed or torn up french bread and move them around with a wooden spoon to get them crisp on all sides, watching so they don't burn, for about 10 minutes. Voila! Homemade croutons.

MAIN:
SPECTACULAR STUFFED
PUMPKIN

Adapted from Dorie Greenspan: "Pumpkin Stuffed with Everything Good"[1]
Serves 8
This recipe is outstanding. Although it may seem crazy to bake a pumpkin like this, it is a very forgiving recipe and a showstopper for any fall gathering!

Ingredients You'll Need

2 medium sugar pie pumpkins, about 3–4 pounds each, cleaned; or 8 smaller sugar pie pumpkins if you want to offer individual servings (Sugar pie pumpkins are not the carving pumpkin variety, but are sweeter and better for baking. They are available seasonally at most grocers.)

2–4 tablespoons butter, softened

Sea salt and freshly ground black pepper, for seasoning

For the Stuffing

2 loaves (around 12 ounces) bread, such as French or sourdough, torn or cut into 1/2-inch cubes

10 slices bacon, cooked and chopped

2 pounds sweet Italian sausage, cooked

2 onions, diced and sautéed

2 apples, such as Granny Smith, diced

3 garlic cloves, minced or pressed

1/2 pound cheese, cubed, such as white cheddar, Gruyère, Quattro Formaggi, or Pepper Jack

1/4 cup green onions, finely chopped

1 cup dried cranberries

1 teaspoon Italian seasoning

2/3 cup heavy cream (or you could use 1/3 cream and 1/3 broth)

1/4 teaspoon ground nutmeg

Tools You'll Need

2 baking sheets
Parchment paper
Knife
Cutting board
Garlic press
Measuring cups
Measuring spoons
Skillet
Tongs
Baking platter or large cutting board
Baking dish (optional)

How to Make It

1. Preheat the oven to 300 degrees Fahrenheit. Line two baking sheets with parchment paper.
2. Cut the bread into 1/2 inch cubes. These don't have to be perfect. Place the cubed bread on a prepared baking sheet, and bake in the preheated oven for 7 minutes. This will dry out the bread to make for a better stuffing.
3. Remove bread from oven and transfer to a large mixing bowl.
4. Raise oven temperature to 450 degrees.
5. Go about cleaning the pumpkins as you would for a jack-o'-lantern. Using a strong knife or a knife from a pumpkin carving set, cut a cap out of the pumpkin tops, large enough to have generous openings to add the stuffing later. Clean out the pumpkins, scraping with a large spoon to remove all pulp and seeds.
6. Take softened butter and divide, spreading around the inside of the pumpkins and then seasoning generously with salt and pepper. Place pumpkins on the prepared baking sheets.
7. Cook the bacon in a skillet on medium-high heat for 10 minutes, turning occasionally with tongs to prevent burning on one side. When done, roughly chop and set aside.
8. While bacon is cooking or when done, heat a skillet to medium-high. Add the sausage (casings removed) and diced onions and apples, along with garlic, and cook for 8–10 minutes. Break the sausage up as you go,

and scrape the pan often to prevent burning. Sausage is done when no pink remains.

9. Add the cooked bacon and cooked sausage mixture to the cubes of bread, along with the cheese, green onions, cranberries, and Italian seasoning. Toss to combine.

10. Measure the cream and mix in nutmeg with the cream. Set aside.

11. Layer the stuffing in the pumpkins in 3 phases, each time adding some cream to each layer. You do not want to soak the mixture, but you do want it sufficiently moist. The pumpkins should be well-stuffed by the end. If there is extra stuffing, you can place it in a greased baking dish and save to bake later, or you can bake it along with the pumpkins for only 30 minutes (at 350 degrees) of the total baking time.

12. Place the caps back on the pumpkins before baking at 450 degrees for 30 minutes. If the pumpkins are browning, cover loosely with foil.

13. After 30 minutes, reduce the heat to 350 and bake for 45 more minutes, removing the pumpkin caps when 20 minutes of bake time remains. This allows excess liquid to evaporate and the stuffing to get nice and bubbly.

14. The pumpkins are done when the flesh pierces easily with a fork.

15. When the pumpkins are done, take extra care when removing from the oven, and transfer to a baking platter or large cutting board. See serving notes below.

Recipe Notes

- Make ahead: The bacon and the sausage can be prepared a day in advance and stored in the refrigerator until ready to use. The bread cubes can be made 2 days in advance and stored in a sealed bag until ready to use.
- When serving, if you are not serving individual pumpkins, then you can take a sharp knife and slice the pumpkins into fourths, serving the stuffing with the pumpkin rind, as it's edible.
- Serving can be fun to do at the table with everyone around because it's not every day people get to see a baked pumpkin!
- Serve on a bed of kale with the cider-maple vinaigrette dressing (recipe below).
- This is also a wonderful holiday stuffing.

SIDE:
KALE SALAD WITH
CIDER-MAPLE VINAIGRETTE

Serves 8

Ingredients You'll Need

>   2 (10-ounce) bags kale, prewashed, trimmed, and shredded (if not, you
>   will have to prep)

For Cider-Maple Vinaigrette
>   2/3 cup olive oil
>   1/3 cup cider vinegar
>   2 tablespoons maple syrup
>   1 tablespoon Dijon mustard
>   1/4 teaspoon sea salt
>   1/8 teaspoon black pepper, freshly ground

Tools You'll Need

>   Salad bowl
>   Whisk

How to Make It

1. Stir all salad dressing ingredients together with a whisk in the bowl you
    plan to use to serve. Toss prepared kale to coat right before dinner is
    ready.

DESSERT:
ANY-FRUIT CRISP WITH
HOMEMADE CARAMEL SAUCE

Serves 16 (I love sending this home with friends for breakfast the next day!)
Apples are the star of this crisp, but you could use any fruit you have on
hand, or combination thereof: strawberries, blackberries, raspberries, blueberries, pears, peaches, or nectarines.

Ingredients You'll Need

> 1/2 cup butter, melted
> 3 large apples (6 cups apples), such as Honeycrisp or Granny Smith,
>   peeled and sliced (For reference, 1 large apple equals 2 cups sliced
>   or chopped.)
> 1 tablespoon lemon juice (half a lemon)
> 1 cup all-purpose flour
> 1 cup granulated sugar
> 3/4 teaspoon sea salt
> 1 teaspoon ground cinnamon
> 1 egg, whisked

For Caramel Sauce
> 1/4 cup water
> 2/3 cup granulated sugar
> 2/3 cup brown sugar
> 1/2 cup butter, softened
> 1 cup heavy cream
> 1 teaspoon vanilla extract
> 1/8 teaspoon sea salt

Optional Garnishes
> Whipped cream
> Vanilla ice cream

Tools You'll Need

> Saucepan
> Microwave-safe dish (optional)

Apple corer (optional)
Vegetable peeler
Knife
Cutting board
Baking dish (9x13 inch)
Citrus juicer (optional)
Mixing bowl
Whisk
Small bowl for egg
Fork
Measuring cups
Measuring spoons
Heatproof spoon

How to Make It

1. Preheat oven to 375 degrees Fahrenheit.
2. In a saucepan or microwave-safe dish, melt the butter. Set aside.
3. Core, peel, and slice apples. If you have an apple corer, that's great to use, but if you don't, just peel the apples with a vegetable peeler and then slice as close to the core as you can.
4. Place apples (or other seasonal fruit) in your baking dish.
5. Sprinkle the lemon juice over the fruit and toss.
6. In a medium mixing bowl, whisk together dry ingredients.
7. Incorporate the whisked egg, tossing with fork until mixture is a crumbly consistency.
8. Sprinkle the flour mixture over fruit. It won't be perfect, but that's what this dessert is all about!
9. Drizzle the melted butter all over the top.
10. Bake 35–40 minutes.
11. Meanwhile, make the sauce. In a small saucepan over high heat, dissolve granulated sugar in the water and mix with a heatproof spoon until it comes to a boil.
12. Reduce heat to medium and stir consistently, waiting for the mixture to turn a light caramel color. This may take up to 15 minutes.
13. When you see the sauce turn the light caramel color, remove from heat and stir in the brown sugar, butter, and heavy cream. This step can cause the caramel to spatter and bubble up, so take care!

14. Stir for 1 minute and place back on medium-high heat to bring to a boil. Reduce heat and simmer the caramel for 3–5 minutes to thicken. If the sugar mixture has clumps, keep stirring until clumps dissolve and become smooth.
15. Remove from the stove top and stir in the vanilla extract and salt.
16. Allow to cool for a few minutes to thicken further.
17. Serve crisp warm with caramel sauce. Add whipped cream and ice cream if you wish!

Recipe Notes

- Make ahead: The caramel sauce can be stored in an airtight container in the refrigerator for a week. Before serving, heat on the stove for a few minutes on medium to get to the right consistency for drizzling.
- The best baking apples are tart-sweet apples like Honeycrisp or Granny Smith.

CHAPTER 11

A Faith for All Seasons

We have been called to heal wounds, to
unite what has fallen apart, and to bring
home those who have lost their way.

—St. Francis of Assisi

The scandals in the Catholic Church have hurt us all. The abhorrent abuse and the steady stream of new allegations, in addition to how things were mishandled or covered up, is sickening and staggering. My heart goes out to those who have been abused and their loved ones; they bear the heaviest burden. For the rest of us, we are impacted by varying degrees, and every time more wrongdoing is pulled into the light, it adds salt to those wounds that never seem to heal.

When the first scandals were unearthed I was a freshman in high school. Back then, I had a very innocent and defensive view of the Church; I knew the abuse was terrible, but I also knew that the Catholic Church was founded by Christ himself, and that nothing could diminish that. As time wore on, I became more aware of just how horrific it all was. Words cannot do it any justice. As the lack of response from those in power grew increasingly deafening, I found my heart growing increasingly dejected. How could God allow this to happen? I felt so many emotions, but above all there was shame. I felt ashamed of crimes I didn't commit, but I felt this for the sake of the Church, who is supposed to be the bulwark of truth and beacon of goodness in the world. How do you proclaim this truth to others when many within have acted in such an evil way?

As the years wore on, it seemed as if people were leaving the Church in droves. Many of my former Catholic schoolmates no longer considered themselves Catholic. Faithful families in my hometown abandoned their parishes of decades for a different denomination of church down the road, but many lost faith altogether. These stories added to the doubts that simmered in my heart, which soon boiled over into despondency. I went through a crisis of faith where I too did not want to go to Mass.

My dad was the one who spoke into my life. He did what good fathers do and listened. I vented my sorrow and frustration (which were not news to him as we had been talking about it for years), but all the same, he was there to validate me, to reassure me that what I felt was real and right. He then offered me advice and encouragement. He exhorted me to go to Mass, saying that for us to turn our backs on the Church was like turning our backs to Jesus on the Cross. This gave me pause. His analogy made everything clear.

Since that day I have had many conversations about the state of the Church with people of every stripe: be it those who left the Church, people who are not Catholic, or people who are Catholic but are angry. The common denominator is that everyone finds the scandals hard to process, let alone understand. Yet it is not for us to understand the heart of darkness. Jesus told us we are meant to be as little children if we are to inherit the kingdom of God. Christ even compared us to sheep—and for good reason. We know sheep are simple animals, but a lesser-known fact is that they are some of the only livestock animals that can do very little to defend themselves. If confronted by a predator, sheep band together and depend on the shepherd for protection; so if a sheep finds itself alone against a predator, that's usually the end of the story.

I'm sure we all can't help but see a striking analogy here. It is in *gathering together* that sheep find safety and strength. Isn't it the same for us? In times like these we must gather together! The predators—the "wolves in sheep's clothing" that scripture warns us about (see Mt 7:15)—want to scatter us. This is ultimately what the devil wants: to break our faith and drive us to isolation. He does everything he can to see us sever our ties with one another and with the Good Shepherd.

So many years ago I was close to choosing isolation, but my spirit was convicted by my father's wisdom. I realized that instead of playing the part of the Bad Thief on Calvary, demanding of Jesus that he do something immediately, I needed to step back and be humble enough to realize that

Jesus is suffering right along with us. God allowed us free will, and that freedom affords the opportunity for wolves to be at large. With this new-found perspective, I knew that in order to heal I needed to reconnect with God. So I decided to show more zeal than I felt—I would go to Mass daily for a year. I offered every Mass I attended for the intention of praying for the departed soul of my Great Aunt Patsy, who had done a lot for me in my college years. This was a powerful antidote to my resentment because it drew me close to God when I would have rather pulled back, and in going to Mass so frequently, I also met a great community of people.

One night, right after the New Year, I heard that a friend I had met from my parish community had just gotten back into town after the death of his father. There was to be a low-key gathering at his apartment to welcome him home and offer condolences. I went with two of my friends and a bottle of wine, not knowing quite what to expect. It turned out to be one of the most warmhearted get-togethers I'll ever remember. Friends had cleaned the man's apartment while he was away and even repainted some walls! It was so touching. We turned on good music, poured the wine, and danced in the living room. Thinking back on that night brings tears to my eyes because there was so much healing in the simple joy of gathering together. In a strange way it was a similar act to that of my dad—it was being present to acknowledge what was lost and to offer encouragement to move forward in faith as best we can.

That is the spirit of the Church we belong to.

Prayer for Gathering

Prayer to St. Michael the Archangel

St. Michael the Archangel, defend us in battle. Be our protection against the wickedness and snares of the devil. May God rebuke him, we humbly pray. And do thou, O Prince of the Heavenly Host, by the power of God, cast into hell Satan and all evil spirits who prowl about the world seeking the ruin of souls. Amen.

Conclude by saying the Our Father.

Prompts for Conversation

- What is one thing you love about being Catholic?
- If you feel comfortable discussing, how did the scandals affect your faith?
- What is one way you can be more involved in your parish?

Menu: Perfect Roast Chicken Dinner

It's arguable that nothing beats roast chicken, and I would argue further that this roast chicken is the best of them all. This menu is a good one to have in the reserves for a dinner party at any time of year, but it works especially well when you're hosting around the holidays. It is not as much work as a Thanksgiving meal by any means, but it is definitely as impressive and good!

Starter: Arugula Cranberry-Orange Salad
Main: Perfect Roast Chicken
Side: Baked Potatoes with Creamy Feta
Dessert: California Carrot Cake

STARTER: ARUGULA CRANBERRY-ORANGE SALAD

Serves 8

Ingredients You'll Need

2 (9-ounce) bags arugula

For Dressing

1 cup olive oil
2/3 cup orange champagne vinegar
2 teaspoons Dijon mustard (not grainy)
2 teaspoons garlic, minced or pressed
Sea salt, to taste
Black pepper, freshly ground, to taste

For Garnish

1 cup green onions, finely chopped
1/2 cup dried cranberries (If you can find orange-flavored, that's best.)

1/2 cup sweet-spicy pecans
1/2 cup shaved Parmesan

Tools You'll Need

Salad serving bowl
Whisk
Measuring cups
Measuring spoons

How to Make It

1. Combine dressing ingredients with a whisk in the bowl you will use to serve the salad, adding salt and pepper to taste.
2. When ready to serve, toss arugula to coat.
3. Sprinkle with green onions, cranberries, pecans, and shaved Parmesan.

MAIN:
PERFECT ROAST CHICKEN

Serves 8

Ingredients You'll Need

2 (5–6-pound) roasting chickens
2 large lemons
2 large garlic cloves, minced or pressed
4 tablespoons butter, softened
2 heaping tablespoons sea salt
Several cranks of freshly ground black pepper
1 cup water or white wine, such as crisp
    Pinot Grigio, Sauvignon Blanc,
    or unoaked Chardonnay (The
    alcohol will evaporate as the
    chicken roasts.)

Tools You'll Need

Paper towel
2 baking dishes (9x13 inch)
Measuring cups
Measuring spoons
Garlic press or knife and cutting board
Fork

How to Make It

Note: Apply all instructions to both chickens. If you are only roasting one chicken, be sure to cut all the ingredient measurements in half.

1. Preheat oven to 425 degrees Fahrenheit.
2. Remove anything in the cavity of the chicken. This is important because there can be an absorbent pad inside the cavity or giblets (little parts of the chicken), which you do not want in there. Rinse the chicken well and then pat dry with a paper towel.
3. Prepare the lemon by piercing with a fork at least 5 times. Set aside.
4. Press or mince the garlic and set aside.
5. Take 2 tablespoons of softened butter and rub all over the chicken skin, getting in between the wings and the thighs. If part of the skin lifts up in any spots, be sure to tuck some butter in there as well. If you have disposable gloves, now is a good time to put them to work!
6. Generously salt and pepper the chicken inside and out.
7. Add garlic and whole lemon to chicken cavity.
8. Place in 9x13 inch baking dish and add 1/2 cup of wine or water to the dish.
9. Roast the chicken for 1 1/2 hours. Once internal temperature has reached 165 degrees, allow it to sit covered under foil for 10 minutes. The juices should run clear when you cut between a leg and thigh.

Recipe Notes

- If the chicken begins to brown too much early on, tent with foil to keep from getting too crisp.
- If you have time, remove your chicken from the refrigerator 30 minutes before you plan to roast. This takes the chill off the bird, and it will cook more evenly.

- A general rule of thumb is to calculate 15–18 minutes of cooking time per pound, plus an additional 15 minutes, plus the 10 minutes resting time. I almost never have to deviate from 1 1/2 hours, plus resting time, but these numbers may help you.

SIDE:
BAKED POTATOES WITH CREAMY FETA

Adapted from Ina Garten: "Crusty Baked Potatoes with Whipped Feta"[1]
Serves 8

Ingredients You'll Need

8 large russet potatoes
2 large lemons, zested
2 heaping tablespoons sea salt
1 teaspoon Italian seasoning
2 tablespoons olive oil

For Creamy Feta
2 blocks (6 ounces) feta cheese, crumbled
1/2 cup sour cream
1/4 cup lemon juice (2 lemons)
2/3 cup olive oil
A few cranks of freshly ground black pepper, to taste

Tools You'll Need

Baking sheet
Aluminum foil
Scrubbing sponge
Measuring cups
Measuring spoons
Grater
Fork
Food processor

How to Make It

1. Preheat oven to 425 degrees Fahrenheit.
2. Prepare a baking sheet with a piece of foil.
3. Wash and dry potatoes. Pierce each potato many times with a fork.
4. Mix together the lemon zest, sea salt, and Italian seasoning.
5. Rub each potato with olive oil and roll in herb mixture.
6. Place on prepared baking sheet and bake for 50–60 minutes. Test with a fork. If a potato pierces easily, they are done; if not, keep in the oven for 5 more minutes and test again.
7. While potatoes bake, start making the creamy feta. Place all ingredients except olive oil in a food processor. Process until smooth for about 30 seconds. Slowly add a stream of olive oil and keep blending until the sauce thickens. Taste and add more sea salt and pepper and lemon if need be.
8. When potatoes pierce easily with a fork, and you are ready to serve, make an incision lengthwise down the center of the potato to create a well for the whipped feta. Add a healthy dollop of whipped feta to each.

DESSERT:
CALIFORNIA CARROT CAKE

Serves 8–10 (generous slices)

This carrot cake is truly a cake for all seasons! It is my husband's favorite cake of all time, so I make it each year for his birthday. The style of this cake was inspired by an oceanside restaurant called Shutters, in Santa Monica, California. My husband and I would occasionally go there to grab a drink and watch the sunset. As guests entered the seating area, there were tempting cakes displayed in glass cloche cake stands: red velvet, blackout cake, and a three-tiered carrot cake with cream-cheese frosting. Needless to say, these cakes were sampled! The carrot cake was as delicious as it looked and had a caramel coating between each of the layers, which I adopted for my own version. If you make the carrot cake once, plan on making it again (and again) by popular demand.

Ingredients You'll Need

    1 tablespoon butter for greasing pans
    2 cups grated carrot (3 carrots)
    2 cups all-purpose flour, plus some for dusting
    2 teaspoons baking soda
    2 teaspoons ground cinnamon
    1/2 teaspoon sea salt
    3 eggs
    2 cups granulated sugar
    3/4 cup coconut oil, melted
    3/4 cup buttermilk
    2 teaspoons vanilla extract
    1 cup flaked coconut
    Sugared walnuts, for garnish
    Edible flowers, for garnish (optional)

For Caramel Glaze

    1/2 cup butter
    1 cup granulated sugar
    1 1/2 teaspoons baking soda
    1/2 cup buttermilk
    1 tablespoon honey or maple syrup
    1 teaspoon vanilla extract

For Cream-Cheese Frosting

    3/4 cup butter, softened
    1 (8-ounce) package cream cheese, softened
    3 cups powdered sugar
    1 1/2 teaspoons vanilla extract

Tools You'll Need

    3 (9-inch) round cake pans
    Parchment paper
    Grater
    Medium mixing bowl
    2 large mixing bowls
    Measuring cups
    Measuring spoons

Handheld or stand mixer
Silicone spatula
Toothpick
Dutch oven or large pot
Spoon or whisk
Sifter (optional)
Wire cooling racks

How To Make It

1. Preheat oven to 350 degrees Fahrenheit.
2. Line 3 (9-inch) round cake pans with parchment paper, lightly buttering and flouring the paper. Set aside.
3. Wash and grate carrots. Measure out your two cups of grated carrots and set aside.
4. In a medium mixing bowl, combine flour, baking soda, cinnamon, and salt.
5. In a large mixing bowl, use your mixer to incorporate eggs, sugar, melted coconut oil, buttermilk, and vanilla on a medium speed until smooth. Slowly add dry mixture at a low speed until just combined.
6. Fold in grated carrot and flaked coconut using a spoon or spatula. Pour batter into prepared cake pans.
7. Bake at 350 degrees for 25 minutes or until a wooden toothpick inserted in center comes out clean. If at 25 minutes it's not ready, test it again in 2-minute increments. I would avoid baking past 30 minutes as it will be overdone.
8. While the cakes are baking, make the caramel glaze and cream-cheese frosting. To make the caramel glaze, place Dutch oven or large pot on the stove. Over medium-high heat, combine all glaze ingredients except vanilla, and bring to a boil, stirring often with a spoon or whisk for 4 minutes. Remove from heat, and stir in vanilla.
9. To make the frosting, use a handheld or stand mixer to combine softened butter and cream cheese until incorporated. Add in (or sift, if possible) powdered sugar and vanilla and mix on a medium-low speed until combined.
10. When cakes are done baking, keep them in the cake pans and place on cooling racks. Allow to cool for 15 minutes before carefully removing

them from the pans and removing the parchment paper from the base of each.

11. Allow to cool 15 minutes more. The cakes should not be warm to the touch when you frost.

12. When ready to frost, keep the cakes on the cooling racks and place parchment underneath. Pour a portion of the caramel on each layer and spread with a spatula to coat, even spreading some on the sides. This stuff is amazing so you can't go wrong here!

13. Transfer the first cake layer to the cake plate you plan to use. Put a dollop of frosting on the top and spread out evenly across. Add the second layer and repeat. Add the third and repeat. Frost the sides in the last step.

14. For garnish, add a sprinkling of flaked coconut, and dot with sugared walnuts around the edge, or edible flowers (available at specialty grocers) are lovely too!

Recipe Notes

• Make ahead: You could grate the carrots the day before and store in an airtight container in the fridge to save on prep time.

CHAPTER 12

Like a Child

Amen, I say to you, unless
you turn and become like
children, you will not enter
the kingdom of heaven.

—Matthew 18:3

God is personal. He is not a far-off experience. He is not a symbol found in landscapes or harvests. He is not an abstract idea. Christianity preaches that God is three persons in one God, and we experience God in concrete through Jesus Christ, who came into this world in order that we might know him and follow him—first, as *a child*. The fact that God became a baby is as affecting as it is astounding. He made himself small so we could hold him. He had no defenses, so we would not put up ours. There was no worldly fanfare surrounding his arrival, so his first adorers were but poor shepherds. Ven. Fulton Sheen said it well:

> Woman gave our Lord His human nature. He asked her to give Him a human life to give Him hands with which to bless children, feet with which to go in search of stray sheep, eyes with which to weep over dead friends, and a body with which to suffer that He might give us a rebirth in freedom and love.[1]

Christ came to suffer and live like one of us in all things but sin. He came to experience the world's hatred in order to raise us up to the heights of freedom and love. Christmas is a call to remember this and meditate on it; the feast is not only a celebration of the historical event of Christ's birth but also a renewed invitation to seek him and accept him.

Christmas strikes the deepest chord in the heart of man, woman, and child. The thrill of hope is in the air, and dark streets are transfigured with the glow of twinkling lights, symbolic of the Light who sparks the weary world's rejoicing. Traditions of gingerbread houses, carols, and peppermint fudge, along with special gatherings and gifting to those near and far, do indeed make the yuletide bright. But these are merely the fruits of the real reason for the season—namely, proclaiming the story of our salvation, and receiving the call to be like a child once more.

So much of Christmas connects with the idea of being childlike. Innocence, hope, and joy—these feelings are on full display when a child receives a long-awaited gift. The wonder and awe is matchless, and it's the purity of heart that makes it so. I remember the Christmases of my early childhood: the gleeful excitement that ensued after hearing sleigh bells jingling outside, which signaled Santa's impending arrival, and subsequently a mad dash to bed, where I whiled away the night watching the seconds drag by on my Lion King alarm clock. The specialness was in the expectation and appreciation of what waited down the staircase. It was a hope bright as a shiny gold coin, but sadly as we grow up this hope can tarnish. We become jaded and spoiled. We forget what it means to have the heart of a child.

In Dickens's timeless classic, *A Christmas Carol*, Ebenezer Scrooge is one so jaded. At the start of the story, his miserly heart is weighed down by the cares of the world, and he has shut out kindness and the appreciation of life's simple pleasures. On Christmas Eve, he has the mystical experience of seeing his life's past, present, and future, and he perceives the grave error in his ways. Come Christmas morning, he leaps out of bed, overjoyed to have a second chance at life. Scrooge vows, "I will honour Christmas in my heart, and try to keep it all the year."[2] His heart, once locked to those who knew him, was now flung open to welcome all he had wronged and rejected, and he became the most generous man anyone knew. This revelation led to his reclamation.

Although we may not be proverbial Scrooges, life can wear away at a soul. It can be a sad feeling to move past childhood and grow older. I felt this when my siblings and I grew up. Christmas was still fun but not quite the same. Then came the first Christmas with a new baby in the family, my daughter. I wanted to visit my family that Christmas, but my baby was just over one month old, so flying wasn't advisable, and the drive was unrealistic at a grueling sixteen hours. But everything is possible at Christmastime. If my husband, baby, and I couldn't go to my family, my family came to us. All eight of them caravanned out to the East Coast a few days after Christmas. Our house was overflowing with family, and there was a never-ending rotation of baby holders! We scheduled her baptism for New Year's Eve, and it was the most joyful celebration. Afterward we gathered together, made honey-baked ham sandwiches and fun finger food, drank a little champagne, and chatted long into the night. All this to celebrate a child.

I have always been a lover of Christmas, but never so much as then. The magnitude of God's act of coming as a babe in swaddling clothes was brought to life for me as I held my little one. My baby was a tangible reminder of what the Christ Child longs to be for us: the object of our affection and joy. The beauty of becoming a child was made clear—not only in the physical sense, but in the spiritual.

Prayer for Gathering

From "In the Bleak Midwinter"

> What can I give Him, poor as I am?
> If I were a shepherd, I would bring a lamb;
> If I were a Wise Man, I would do my part;
> Yet what I can I give Him: give my heart.

Conclude by saying the Our Father.

Prompts for Conversation

- What is your favorite Christmas memory?
- In what way can you be more childlike in your faith?
- What makes having childlike faith difficult for you?

Menu:
Pizza Party and Cookie Swap

One of the long-standing Christmas traditions in my family is to have a pizza party and then watch *Home Alone* for a movie night. This menu is inspired by that tradition. People will love sampling the Christmas punch while the pizzas bake in the oven (my secret is prebaked crusts!). And for dessert, encouraging a festive cookie swap is a fun way to get everyone in the Christmas spirit.

Starter: Christmas Punch
Main: Three Pizzas, Three Different Ways: Meat Lover's Pizza, Southwestern Pizza with Avocado Crema, Mediterranean Pizza with Pomegranate Molasses
Side: Green Salad with Lemon Dressing
Dessert: Gingersnap Cookies

STARTER:
CHRISTMAS PUNCH

Serves 8

Ingredients You'll Need

1 pint raspberry sorbet, softened
1/2 cup orange juice, freshly squeezed (2 oranges)
1/4 cup, plus 2 tablespoons granulated sugar
1 (28-ounce) bottle ginger ale, chilled (or 4 [6.8-ounce] bottles)
1 (32-ounce) cranberry juice, chilled (not juice cocktail)
Pomegranate seeds, for garnish (optional)

Tools You'll Need

Large pitcher or punch bowl
Ladle (if you're using a punch bowl)

Citrus juicer (optional)
Knife (optional)
Cutting board (optional)
Large spoon
Measuring cups
Measuring spoons
Small ice cream scoop

How to Make It

1. Soften the pint of raspberry sorbet by allowing it to sit on the counter for 20 minutes.
2. Juice the oranges. In a pinch you could use store-bought orange juice for this!
3. In a large pitcher or punch bowl, combine the orange juice and sugar, stirring until sugar is dissolved.
4. Pour the ginger ale and cranberry juice into the pitcher and gently stir to mix.
5. Take a small ice cream scoop, and add 1 scoop of sorbet to each glass before you pour the punch. Sprinkle with pomegranate seeds for garnish if you have them. Serve right away!

Recipe Notes

- Make ahead: You may assemble the punch in advance on the day of the gathering, but do not add the ginger ale until the last minute to prevent it from going flat.

MAIN:
THREE PIZZAS, THREE DIFFERENT WAYS

Serving Note: Each pizza serves eight. If you have a gathering of eight, I recommend making two pizzas so people can help themselves to another slice!

MAIN PIZZA ONE:
MEAT LOVER'S PIZZA

Serves 8

Ingredients You'll Need

1 prebaked 12-inch pizza crust or flatbread
1 pound spicy or sweet Italian sausage, casings removed
1 yellow or white onion, sliced
2 cloves garlic, minced or pressed
1 teaspoon Italian seasoning
Sea salt, to taste
Black pepper, freshly ground, to taste
1 (16-ounce) jar of pizza sauce
1 (5-ounce) package pepperonis
1 (4-ounce) can black olives, sliced
1 (8-ounce) block fresh mozzarella
1/4 teaspoon red pepper flakes (for garnish)

Tools You'll Need

Knife
Cutting board
Measuring cups
Measuring spoons
Can opener
Baking sheet
Skillet
Heatproof spoon or meat turner
Spoon

How to Make It

1. Preheat oven to 450 degrees Fahrenheit. Check your pizza crust package instructions in case it recommends a different temperature for the specific kind of crust you purchased.

2. Heat a large skillet on the stove at medium-high heat. Add sausages without the casings, and with a heatproof spoon or meat turner, break them into chunks, moving around frequently. Cook until no pink remains, about 10 minutes. Drain grease into a heatproof container, and as always, a friendly reminder to be extra careful and to never put grease down your drain. Remove cooked sausage to large bowl and set aside.

3. In the freshly degreased skillet, sauté the onion for 5 minutes on medium-high heat, until onions are translucent. Add crushed garlic and sauté for 30 more seconds. Add onion and garlic to sausage mixture along with Italian seasoning and salt and pepper to taste.

4. Using a spoon, spread half the pizza sauce onto the prebaked pizza crust. If it looks like it needs more, add in small increments, but you don't want the crust to get too soggy.

5. Using a spoon, spread the sausage mixture evenly over the pizza sauce.

6. Place a layer of pepperonis and the black olives on top.

7. Add chunks of the fresh mozzarella all over the pizza. There is no wrong way to do this!

8. Place pizza on baking sheet and bake for 12–15 minutes, or until heated through and golden.

9. At the last minute, broil to get extra crispy, but watch carefully so it does not burn.

10. Add red pepper flakes for garnish. Slice and serve!

MAIN PIZZA TWO: SOUTHWESTERN PIZZA WITH AVOCADO CREMA

Serves 8

Ingredients You'll Need

1 prebaked 12-inch pizza crust
Sea salt, to taste
Black pepper, freshly ground, to taste
2 tablespoons olive oil
1 pound chicken tenders
3–4 jalapeños, seeded and sliced
1 (14.5-ounce) can refried black beans
2 cloves garlic, minced or pressed
1/4 cup lime juice (2 limes)
1/2 teaspoon cumin
1/2 teaspoon onion powder
1/4 teaspoon cayenne pepper
1 green pepper, sliced
1 onion, thinly sliced
1/2 cup cheese, such as Monterey Jack or chèvre

For Avocado Crema

1 large avocado, pitted
1/4 cup coconut milk (full fat)
1 lime, zested and juiced
1/4 teaspoon sea salt
1/8 teaspoon garlic powder
2 tablespoons extra virgin olive oil or avocado oil
Black pepper, freshly ground, to taste

Tools You'll Need

Knife
Cutting board
Measuring cups
Measuring spoons

Can opener
Baking sheet
Skillet
Tongs
Heatproof spoon
Citrus juicer (optional)
Spoon
Grater or zester
Food processor

How to Make It

1. Preheat oven to 450 degrees Fahrenheit. Check your pizza crust package instructions in case it recommends a different temperature for the specific kind of crust you purchased.
2. Salt and pepper chicken tenders. Place large skillet on stove top. Add 1 tablespoon olive oil and heat on medium-high heat until shimmering. Add the chicken tenders, and cook on each side for 5–6 minutes or until chicken is no longer pink and the juices run clear. Once cooked, allow chicken to cool for 5 minutes, and then cut into bite-sized pieces.
3. Wash, deseed, and slice the fresh jalapeños. Friendly reminder: never touch your eyes after handling jalapeños, and use disposable gloves if you have them.
4. Make the bean paste in a small saucepan. On stove top over medium heat, use a heatproof spoon to combine the refried black beans, garlic, lime juice, cumin, onion powder, and cayenne. Stir until combined and heated through, about 5 minutes. Salt and pepper to taste.
5. Next, seed and slice green pepper. Slice onion.
6. Take another pan or skillet and heat 1 tablespoon of olive oil on medium-high heat. Add sliced pepper and onion to pan and sauté until tender, about 5–7 minutes. Remove from heat.
7. Using a spoon, spread bean paste evenly over your prepared pizza crust.
8. On top of the bean paste, sprinkle cooked chicken, onion, green pepper, and jalapeño slices. (Do not feel as if you have to use all the ingredients if the pizza is getting overloaded. You can save any leftover ingredients to have in a salad or as a veggie mix the next day.)

9. Place pizza on baking sheet and bake pizza for 10 minutes and then remove from oven to sprinkle with cheese of choice. Cook 5 more minutes or until cheese is melted and pizza is golden.

10. While pizza is in the oven, pit the avocado and make the crema. Using a food processor, pulse the avocado, coconut milk, lime zest and juice, sea salt, and garlic powder for up to 1 minute or until smooth. Slowly add 2 tablespoons of olive oil or avocado oil in a thin stream while processing, for around 30 seconds, as it starts to thicken. Give a few cranks of black pepper and taste for seasoning.

11. Drizzle crema on finished pizza, slice, and serve!

Recipe Notes

- This pizza can easily be transformed into a nondairy or vegetarian pizza. Just omit the chicken and cheese and use a nondairy cheese substitute, while keeping the same veggie ingredients.

MAIN PIZZA THREE: MEDITERRANEAN PIZZA WITH POMEGRANATE MOLASSES

Serves 8

Time Note: The pomegranate molasses takes 1 1/2 hours to make, including stove time and set time. Be sure to make it in advance.

Ingredients You'll Need

1 prebaked 12-inch pizza crust
1 cup hummus
1 teaspoon Italian seasoning
1/4 teaspoon red pepper flakes
1 small red onion, thinly sliced
3/4 cup feta cheese, crumbled
1/2 cup sun-dried tomatoes, chopped
1/2 cup Kalamata olives, pitted and chopped

For Pomegranate Molasses
   4 cups (32-ounces) pomegranate juice
   1/2 cup, plus 1 heaping tablespoon granulated sugar
   4 tablespoons lemon juice (2 lemons)

Tools You'll Need

   Baking sheet
   Knife
   Cutting board
   Measuring cups
   Measuring spoons
   Citrus juicer (optional)
   Saucepan
   Spoon

How to Make It

1. Preheat oven to 450 degrees Fahrenheit. Check your pizza crust package instructions in case it recommends a different temperature for the specific kind of crust you purchased.
2. In a small bowl, combine hummus with the Italian seasoning and red pepper flakes. Spread evenly over crust.
3. Sprinkle red onion, feta, sun-dried tomatoes, and Kalamata olives on the crust.
4. Place pizza on baking sheet and bake 12–15 minutes or until golden.
5. For the pomegranate molasses, in a saucepan over medium-high heat, bring the pomegranate juice, sugar, and lemon juice to boil; reduce heat to medium-low.
6. Allow the juice mixture to simmer (uncovered) for 45 minutes, stirring every few minutes to keep the sugar from sticking and burning on the bottom of pan.
7. After 45 minutes the juice will be reduced significantly. Lower the heat and continue to simmer for 15 minutes.
8. The mixture should be close to done after the hour is up. To test, take a spoon and dip it into the liquid. If it coats the spoon, then the molasses is done.

9. Allow the molasses to cool for at least 30 minutes. During the cooling process it will continue to thicken. Store in an airtight container in the refrigerator until ready to use. Then drizzle over the pizza to serve.

Recipe Notes

- Make ahead: You can keep pomegranate molasses in an airtight container in the refrigerator for up to 6 months.
- This recipe produces 1 cup of pomegranate molasses.

SIDE:
GREEN SALAD WITH LEMON DRESSING

Serves 8

Ingredients You'll Need

2 (9-ounce) bags lettuce, such as spring greens, romaine, or arugula

For Dressing

1/2 cup olive oil
1/2 cup lemon juice (3 large lemons or 4 medium)
2 tablespoons Dijon mustard
2 cloves garlic, minced or pressed
2 teaspoons honey
1 teaspoon Italian seasoning
1/8 teaspoon sea salt
Black pepper, freshly ground, to taste

Tools You'll Need

Salad serving bowl
Whisk

How to Make It

1. Combine all dressing ingredients in the salad serving bowl and whisk away! Add lettuce and toss salad when ready to serve.

Recipe Notes
- Make ahead: This dressing stores for 1 week in the refrigerator. It goes with practically everything!

DESSERT:
GINGERSNAP COOKIES

Yields 24

This is a recipe that my Grandma Fowler gave to my mother, and so the cookies have been dubbed "Famous Fowler Gingersnaps." My family would always have these growing up (and still do). Even though gingersnaps could be pigeonholed as an autumn-to-Christmas cookie, I personally reject that stereotype—these are perfect year-round! Gingersnaps are easy to make and are a yummy little gift-basket treat for anyone. They are also very delicious frozen (and then dunked in coffee!).

Ingredients You'll Need

1 1/2 cups butter, softened
2 1/4 cups granulated sugar, divided
1/4 cup molasses
2 eggs
4 cups all-purpose flour
3 teaspoons baking soda
2 teaspoons ground cinnamon
2 teaspoons ground ginger
1 teaspoon ground cloves
1 teaspoon sea salt

Tools You'll Need

Baking sheet
Parchment paper
Measuring cups
Measuring spoons
Handheld or stand mixer
Sifter (optional)

Large mixing bowl
Small mixing bowl

How to Make It

1. Preheat oven to 350 degrees Fahrenheit and line a baking sheet with parchment paper. Set aside.
2. With a handheld or stand mixer, cream the butter and 2 cups of sugar, adding molasses and eggs until just incorporated.
3. Combine (and if possible, sift) dry ingredients (except remaining sugar) in a large mixing bowl, and add to butter mixture.
4. Place the remaining 1/4 cup of sugar in a small mixing bowl.
5. Form dough into balls the size of large walnuts, and roll them in the prepared sugar bowl.
6. Place the prepped gingersnaps on the prepared cookie sheet, and bake for 8–10 minutes. The cookies are done when they are set but still soft, as they will firm up as they cool.

Entertaining Tips

Do not neglect hospitality,
for through it some have
unknowingly entertained angels.

—Hebrews 13:2

The word *entertain* comes from Latin and originally meant "to maintain" or "to continue." How fitting! In order to maintain and foster our earthly relationships, we must entertain. By the fifteenth century the word donned a new meaning, "to show hospitality." When we show hospitality to others, we exhibit generosity of spirit by setting ourselves aside to serve them. This mindset affords us countless opportunities to show Christian love to every person who enters the place we each call home, be they a family member, a friend, or a new acquaintance.

Anyone who has ever hosted a gathering knows that entertaining takes effort, which is why there are industries dedicated to pulling off events both great and small. To serve can sometimes feel like a burden (especially when you're up late at night making something for the day ahead and it feels as if there are miles to go before you sleep!). But St. John Paul II had something to say about this kind of love and service.

> Mary called herself the "handmaid of the Lord" (Luke 1:38). . . .
> Putting herself at God's service, she also put herself at the service
> of others: a service of love. Precisely through this service Mary
> was able to experience in her life a mysterious, but authentic
> "reign." It is not by chance that she is invoked as "queen of heaven
> and earth." The entire community of believers thus invokes her;
> many nations and peoples call upon her as their "queen." For her,
> "to reign" is to serve! Her service is "to reign!"[1]

153

What a beautiful sentiment to keep close when we are in the midst of acting in the place of the busy St. Martha to those we love. Whether we're hosting a gathering for a birthday party or baby shower, or baking cookies for family, make no mistake—there's nothing lowly in our service.

I love thinking of St. Martha as a model for service. It is noted twice in the New Testament that Martha was a lady who cared for those around her. She "served" (Jn 12:2; cf. Lk 10:40). This is best illustrated in the well-known story recorded in scripture when Jesus came to visit the house of Martha, Mary, and Lazarus (see Lk 10:38–42). As the story goes, Martha is playing hostess, worried about taking care of everyone (her guest of honor is Jesus no less!), while her sister Mary sits at the feet of Jesus, being no help to her at all. Martha was busy caring for everyone but herself. How many times can we relate to this? How many times does it feel as if we're missing the fun "Mary" moments because there's a work project that needs to be finished, a kitchen that needs to be cleaned, a meal that needs to be made—our lists go on and on. No doubt Martha would have preferred sitting at the feet of Jesus, but she had reality to deal with—after all, dinner wasn't going to make itself! Jesus gives her a gentle reprimand, though. As she is stressing and complaining to Jesus, he acknowledges that she is worried about many things, but that Mary has chosen the better part. So what is the "better part" specifically? I don't think it necessarily means sitting down and not working; rather, it means to be fully and intentionally present to Jesus and those around us. This is such a challenge, especially in our time-poor, distraction-saturated world. But it is possible. Even though we often play Martha to those around us, we can have the heart of Mary while we work. Yes, as St. John Paul II said, "'to reign' is to serve!"

In this spirit, the following gathering etiquette tips offer ideas to help raise your gathering game. While some things may not apply to your gatherings (you may not be concerned about fancy dishware!), they are intended to help add extra touches of care and consideration when hosting the ones you love.

Invitation

Notifying people in advance of a gathering is important for securing a space on everyone's schedule. For the casual gatherings at the heart of this book, it is nice to give an invitation one to two weeks in advance, whether that's via call, text, social media, email, or snail mail. For more formal affairs, such as a baby shower, four weeks in advance is the standard.

Allergies

Once you've set a date for your gathering and have invited your guests, it is considerate to inquire about any allergies or special dietary needs. Is someone allergic to shrimp? Does someone avoid dairy? Is someone gluten-free? This is all-important to know before building your menu. Depending on the special requirement, you may be able to easily modify recipes accordingly. For instance, if someone has a dairy-free diet and there is cheese in the salad and on the main entrée, you can serve the cheese on the side for the salad, and you can omit the cheese on a portion of the entrée that will be designated for your guest. Oftentimes, you do not need to overhaul the entire menu in order to make the necessary and thoughtful adjustments for your guest.

Your List

Making a general to-do list for everything you need to get done before the gathering is tremendously helpful. To quote an old choir teacher: "Amateurs try to remember; professionals write it down." Writing down the ingredients you need at the store will hopefully save you from making the return trip for a forgotten ingredient (always my Achilles' heel!). Writing down everything you need to do—from borrowing extra chairs from a friend, to setting the table—will keep things on track.

Lighting

Lighting sets the mood. For the best ambiance, turn down all ceiling lighting (unless it can be dimmed), and rely on lamplight to illuminate your space. Candles serve as beautiful accents, both as adornments for the tablescape and as sources of light throughout. If outdoors, try stringing festoon lights overhead the central gathering area. These are inexpensive and add so much warmth and character.

Fragrance

A high-quality scented candle is worth every penny. Light the candle one hour before guests arrive to fill the air with fragrance. It's nice to have scents that complement the time of year: for the winter, vanilla or amber; for spring, lemon or orange blossom; for summer, rose and black currant; for fall, pumpkin and cinnamon. Fig is a subtle scent that is perfect all year round. Nothing is so inviting as entering a home with a lovely aroma!

Music

Music is as important for the gathering prep as it is for the gathering itself! Put on a playlist that you love while you are prepping for people to arrive. Mellow music playing in the background can keep things cool even when you're in the throes of making a menu come to life. To set the tone for the gathering, select a playlist and keep the volume low enough to allow conversation to be heard, but loud enough to create atmosphere. Playing it over a speaker is ideal—you don't need anything fancy; a little speaker can do the job nicely. Experiment with different genres: jazz, French radio, nineties love songs, big band. If you have a record player, have guests bring their favorite vinyl.

Edit the Scene

In film, to prepare a scene for the camera is to "edit the scene." This is when you make sure there are no stray water bottles, pieces of equipment, or other miscellaneous things lying around that shouldn't be in the shot. I always "edit the scene" before a gathering, even if it means putting clutter in a laundry basket and putting that behind closed doors!

Foliage and Flora

Having a pop of green in your space cheers up any room. If you're not a green thumb (like me), there are many fantastic faux options available to spruce up your space. I also like to add a festive splash of sparkle to greenery. Try adding Christmas lights to a fig tree, and see the transformation that takes place (I keep mine twinkling year-round!). Fresh flowers also add an essential touch of elegance, and for me they are a must for any get-together. The easiest way to arrange a stunning bouquet is to buy three bunches of the same flower. For this idea, you could use the same color, such as an array of pristine white roses or a gorgeous grouping of canary gladioli. If you want to mix it up, you could work within a color palette, such as three bunches of carnations in baby pink, magenta, and fuchsia, or different hues of hydrangea with dramatic sprigs of eucalyptus. It's a simple way to make a big statement! Try buying fresh flowers the day before at a warehouse club, supermarket, or a local farmer's market to avoid breaking the bank. To keep your flowers fresh, fill your vase with cool water, mixed with 2 tablespoons of vinegar and 2 tablespoons of sugar. Then, remove all the foliage on stems that would be below the waterline, and cut the bottom of the stems at an angle before placing them into the water. If your flowers start to wilt, trim the stems and place in one inch of boiling water (110 degrees Fahrenheit) for 30 seconds before placing them back in your vase, prepared with fresh cool water with the vinegar and sugar mixture. This trick should restore a healthy bloom!

Powder Room

As guests may need the powder room, it's thoughtful to have it sparkling clean. Hand soap, fresh hand towels, plenty of toilet paper, and a little scented candle are must-haves.

Refreshment

A great way to make people feel welcome right away is to offer them a refreshment. Sparkling water, wine, and beer are can't-miss offerings. Also, on the beverage front, serving water with dinner is always necessary, even if people have an alternative beverage from earlier in the evening. Have glasses on the table, and fill them before dinner is served.

Tablescape

The table should be a place of welcome and festivity. No matter the gathering, it's best to err on the side of relaxed and friendly, rather than rigid and staid. Seating doesn't have to match, but make sure each guest has a chair when it comes time to sit. The table centerpiece options are endless and can vary by season. For the Christmas holidays, try weaving fresh evergreen in between mercury votive candles and bottlebrush trees (maybe a sparkly reindeer here and there too!). For spring, an array of pastel-colored flowers mixed in with a strand of brightly colored eggs, twisted in eucalyptus and lavender, makes for a lovely display; also, sprinkling chocolate-foil eggs around the tablescape never goes unappreciated! For summer, you can use lemon leaves with mini-twinkle lights in mason jars (to mimic fireflies) with brightly colored garden roses and sunflowers. For autumn, try hollowing out a pumpkin and using it as your flower vase, with squash and mini pumpkins placed about the table with a scattering of candy corn for a burst of extra color. If all else fails, bunches of flowers in non-traditional vases (ceramic, mason jars) and unscented taper candles add loads of charm.

Linens

Napkins are a necessity, but if you want to take it to the next level, opt for linen napkins. These instantly elevate any table setting and can be very inexpensive, especially if you watch for sales and buy up then. You can never go wrong with a classic neutral, or you can mix and match colors for fun! Along the same lines, a nicely pressed tablecloth is an easy way to add a touch of class to any table.

Place Settings

Place settings are not only a lovely way to make things personal for your guests, but they also serve as seating direction and create opportunities for everyone to meet new people. Try tying homemade name tags to a fresh sprig of herbs, or attach them to a little gift such as a brown seed packet of chocolate-covered sunflower seeds. These don't have to be perfectly done but can add so much personality!

Dinnerware

Fine china can mean different things for different people. Maybe you want a classic pattern in matching place settings, or maybe you want to collect different pieces at antique marts over time. You could even create your very own set in a pottery class! It may take time, but the end result will be full of character and provide such a great story. In the interim, as you build up to a full set of proper place settings, you can use paper plates or buy less expensive dishes that you can repurpose as everyday dishes once you complete your dream set. It doesn't have to be expensive to look nice.

Cutlery

Having nice silverware is another investment piece to consider; it's not only a nice touch for gatherings, but it has everyday value for you. There's the option to go the vintage route, but if you want a recommendation for something new, a great brand is Liberty Tabletop. They have pretty patterns that cross over perfectly from casual to formal. It's also the only flatware that's made in the USA.

Glassware

Glassware is something that is very easy to find secondhand. Watch for estate sales, and you may find yourself landing some gorgeous crystal at a bargain-basement price. I was lucky enough to receive glassware from my husband's grandmother. She also surprised us with Waterford wine glasses for our wedding, which turned out to be the best gift! The glasses are all one size and make a statement with pretty etching on the side, so we decided against getting different glasses for specific wines. This keeps things simple, and everyone always comments on how exquisite they are. So, try a unique multipurpose wine glass for the win.

Platters and Serving Bowls

Large platters and serving bowls come in handy for gatherings of all sizes. It can be fun to get an assortment of styles to suit different occasions: colorful, plain, classic, quirky, marble, or wooden—perfect for everything from cheese boards to pastas. Big serving dishes save you from having to plate individual food when that's not the style in which you're serving. Display your platters and bowls on the counter, serving buffet, or even another table in order to create a serving line for your guests. This is often better than serving "family style" at the table, which tends to devolve into endless passing requests that can make it feel like a boardinghouse, which is something to avoid!

Seasoning

Seasoning is everything when it comes to cooking. As they say, you can always add, but can't take away, so it's best to be judicious and then taste as you go to adjust the seasonings before serving—which is always the fun part! Oftentimes salt, butter, and other rich ingredients get a bad name, but they add flavor and goodness to meals in a special way. Gatherings can be the perfect time to indulge in these delicious treats.

Prayer before Meal

Before eating your meal, respectfully ask people to pause for a prayer. You can never go wrong with the mainstay of "Bless us, O Lord, and these, thy gifts, which we are about to receive from thy bounty. Through Christ, our Lord. Amen." To make it more personal, you can add a few words of thanksgiving for those present, for the relationships you share, and for God to bless the food and conversation. Prayer before meals is good practice even if guests are not of your faith. The way you present your home and personal practices are opportunities to share the Light of Christ with others. This extends into having religious art in your home, such as a blessed crucifix, a statue of Our Lady, or a picture of the Sacred Heart, to name a few. Celebrating our Catholic faith openly makes our lives the equivalent of beautiful churches. We might be the only "church" someone ever encounters.

Gifting

When you attend a gathering, it is thoughtful to bring a little thank-you for your host or hostess. A bottle of nice wine never fails, but if you want to get creative, you could bring something along the lines of good extra virgin olive oil, truffle oil, fine chocolate, or fancy honey.

The Day Before

In a perfect world (which of course none of us live in) it's great to have almost everything done in advance of guests arriving, especially when you're hosting all by yourself. Below are a few ideas to help alleviate the workload on the day-of, especially since gatherings don't happen in a vacuum and we all have work, family, and outside commitments contending with our party-planning schedules.

- Make a to-do list.
- Shop for all your dry goods up to a week before and for the fresh items the day before.
- Clean what needs to be cleaned (powder room, etc.).
- Prepare all food that can be made in advance.
- Set the table (as long as you won't be using it beforehand!).
- Set out the platters you plan to use for serving in the order you would like the serving line to progress, and write your dishes on Post-it notes; then stick them on the corresponding serving dishes. This eliminates guesswork at the last minute and being short on serving dishes when you're ready to serve.
- Set out the serving utensils you will need next to each serving platter.
- Buy and arrange flowers.
- Above all, have fun!

Pantry Staples

As you cook, you build an arsenal of all sorts of staples in the kitchen. While some recipes call for very specific ingredients, many things come up frequently enough that it can be helpful to have them on hand at all times and even a few backups in reserve!

Refrigerated

Butter, salted
Cheese (whatever type you use most)
Cream cheese
Eggs
Half-and-half or heavy cream
Milk
Mustard, yellow and Dijon
Sour cream
Yogurt (plain, full-fat as a substitute for sour cream)

Frozen

French bread, to thaw
Puff pastry, to thaw

Produce

Garlic cloves
Lemons
Limes
Onions, white or yellow

Dry Goods

Active dry yeast
All-purpose flour
Baking powder
Baking soda
Beef stock cubes
Brown sugar
Chicken stock cubes
Chocolate chips
Cocoa powder, unsweetened
Dry pasta of choice
Granulated sugar
Powdered sugar

Canned Goods

Beans
Crushed tomatoes
Corn
Coconut milk (full-fat, as a substitute for dairy in some recipes)
Tomato sauce
Nutella

Spices, Seasonings, and Condiments

Cayenne pepper
Celery salt
Cloves
Cumin
Garlic powder
Garlic salt
Ginger
Ground cinnamon
Ground nutmeg
Hot sauce (such as Tabasco)
Italian seasoning
Mustard
Onion powder

Pepper (ground)

Peppercorns in a pepper mill (to have freshly ground pepper)

Red pepper flakes

Sea salt (I recommend sea salt in all my recipes. If you only have table salt on hand, use a little less than recommended since it is processed salt and has more iodine, which results in a slightly metallic flavor.)

Vanilla extract

Oils and Vinegars

Balsamic vinegar

Cider vinegar

Coconut oil (as a butter alternative in some recipes)

Extra virgin olive oil (for salad dressings; unsafe to use at high smoke points)

Olive oil (safe to use for sautéing and in the oven)

Red wine vinegar

White wine vinegar

Tools of the Trade

You don't need a registry at Williams-Sonoma to have what it takes to make great food! The items below are those I reach for most consistently when I'm preparing meals and are readily available at reasonable prices. This is not to say you need all of these tools at once to make a dish, but you may find them helpful additions to your collection of kitchenware as you spend more time cooking and baking.

Basics

Aluminum foil
Baking dish (8x8 inch)
Baking dish (9x13 inch)
Baking sheets (rimmed) or jelly roll pans (2, around 12x18 inches)
Box grater
Bread loaf pan (9x5 inch)
Cake pans (2, 8-inch)
Can opener
Citrus juicer
Colander
Cutting boards (small and large)
Garlic press
Handheld mixer
Heatproof glass measuring cup (This is perfect for heating things in the microwave or for holding the drained hot grease from meat.)
Heatproof meat turner (great for browning meat)
Hot pads
Measuring cups
Measuring spoons
Meat thermometer

Oven mitts
Parchment paper
Pastry brush
Pie plate (9-inch)
Pot (large) or Dutch oven (at least 5 1/2-quart capacity)
Potato masher
Rolling pin
Saucepan (medium)
Scissors (dedicated for kitchen use)
Sifter or sieve
Silicone spatulas, heatproof (2)
Skillets (small and large)
Slotted spoon
Soup ladle (large)
Tongs (2)
Toothpicks
Vegetable peeler
Wax paper
Whisk
Wine corkscrew
Wooden spoons
Zester

Investment Pieces

Braiser (2 1/4 quart capacity) —This is amazing for cooking meat and
   a variety of other dishes.
Dutch oven (5 1/2 quart capacity) —I recommend this item above all
   others. My first Dutch oven was a persimmon-colored Cuisinart
   for fifty dollars from the Santa Monica TJ Maxx. I used it almost
   every day for years! I finally got a Le Creuset, and the higher quality
   leaves me with no regrets.
Stand mixer
Food processor
Quality knives (vegetables, paring, bread)

Notes

Chapter 1: Walk On Securely

1. Mother Mary Francis, P.C.C., "Eternal Values" (Chapter conference presentation for the Poor Clares in Roswell, NM), accessed March 4, 2018, http://poorclares—roswell.org/eternalvalues.html.

Chapter 2: The Heart of Dating

1. *The Dating Project*, directed by Jon Cipiti, performances by Kerry Cronin and Chris Meehan (Los Angeles: Mpower Pictures, 2017).

2. Society of the Little Flower, "Miraculous Invocation to St. Thérèse," https://blog.littleflower.org/prayers/miraculous-invocation-to-st-therese/.

3. Ree Drummond, "Braised Short Ribs," *The Pioneer Woman*, March 7, 2011, https://thepioneerwoman.com/cooking/short-ribs-in-tomato-sauce/.

Chapter 3: A Sweet Story

1. The Free Dictionary, s.v. "satisfaction (*n.*)," accessed April 23, 2020, https://www.thefreedictionary.com/satisfaction.

2. Daniel P. Jamros, "Satisfaction for Sin: Aquinas on the Passion of Christ," *Irish Theological Quarterly* 56, no. 4 (December 1, 1990): 307–28.

Chapter 5: Closer to Eden

1. Gary D. Chapman, *The Five Love Languages: How to Express Heartfelt Commitment to Your Mate* (Chicago: Northfield, 1995).

2. Ina Garten, "Curried Chicken Salad," *Barefoot Contessa Family Style: Easy Ideas and Recipes That Make Everyone Feel Like Family: A Cookbook* (New York: Clarkson Potter, 2002), 61.

Chapter 8: Time to Gather

1. Don Stewart, "Why Did God Reject Cain's Sacrifice?," *Blue Letter Bible*, accessed April 16, 2020, https://www.blueletterbible.org/faq/don_stewart/don_stewart_714.cfm.

2. Rhitu Chatterjee, "Americans Are a Lonely Lot, and Young People Bear the Heaviest Burden," NPR, May 1, 2018, https://www.npr.org/sections/health-shots/2018/05/01/606588504/americans-are-a-lonely-lot-and-young-people-bear-the-heaviest-burden.

Chapter 9: Eternal Wealth

1. *Yours, Mine and Ours*, directed by Melville Shavelson, performances by Lucille Ball, Henry Fonda (Los Angeles: Desilu Productions, 1968).

2. This version of the prayer appears on EWTN's website as "Mother Teresa's Prayer for the Family." https://www.ewtn.com/catholicism/devotions/mother-teresas-prayer-for-the-family-352.

3. Joanna Gaines, "Jo's Quick Table Salad," *Magnolia Table: A Collection of Recipes for Gathering* (New York: HarperCollins, 2018), 127.

4. Suzanne Fowler, "Golden Glazed Chicken," *Building the Family Cookbook* (Seattle: Iona Publishing, 2003), 228.

5. Deb Perelman, "Salted Brown Butter Crispy Treats," *Smitten Kitchen*, November 2, 2009, https://smittenkitchen.com/2009/11/salted-brown-butter-crispy-treats/.

Chapter 10: Travelers

1. Dorie Greenspan, "Pumpkin Stuffed with Everything Good," *Around My French Table: More Than 300 Recipes from My Home to Yours* (Boston: Houghton Mifflin Harcourt, 2010), 364.

Chapter 11: A Faith for All Seasons

1. Ina Garten, "Crusty Baked Potatoes with Whipped Feta," *Make It Ahead Cookbook* (New York: Clarkson Potter, 2014), 154–55.

Chapter 12: Like a Child

1. Fulton J. Sheen, *The World's First Love: Mary, Mother of God* (San Francisco: Ignatius Press, 2010), 73.

2. Charles Dickens, *A Christmas Carol* (London, 1843).

Entertaining Tips

1. Pope John Paul II, "Letter to Women for Beijing Conference," July 10, 1995, https://www.ewtn.com/catholicism/library/papal-letter-to-women-8640.

Ingredient Index

Catherine Fowler Sample wrote and produced the award-winning documentary *The Dating Project*, for which she appeared on a number of Catholic radio and television stations, including EWTN, CatholicTV, and Relevant Radio. She is a former production executive at Mpower Pictures, where she wrote and produced two faith-based curriculums on dating and relationships and worked on multiple films, including *The Drop Box* and *Emanuel*. Fowler Sample also has served as a writer and producer on projects for Family Theater Productions and Focus on the Family. She speaks nationally to Catholic audiences on dating and relationships.

Fowler Sample earned a bachelor's degree in communication studies with an emphasis on film and electronic arts from California State University Long Beach. She lives with her family in Charlotte, North Carolina.

AVE

AVE MARIA PRESS

Founded in 1865, Ave Maria Press,
a ministry of the Congregation of
Holy Cross, is a Catholic publishing
company that serves the spiritual and
formative needs of the Church and its
schools, institutions, and ministers;
Christian individuals and families; and
others seeking spiritual nourishment.

For a complete listing of titles from

Ave Maria Press

Sorin Books

Forest of Peace

Christian Classics

visit www.avemariapress.com

AVE MARIA PRESS
Notre Dame, IN
A Ministry of the United States Province of Holy Cross